God's
OK-
You're
OK?

Perspectives on Christian Worship

by R. W. Baynes

You may obtain a 64-page leader's guide to accompany this paperback. Order number 40089 from Standard Publishing or your local supplier.

A Division of Standard Publishing
Cincinnati, Ohio 45231
No. 40088

Scripture quotations are from the King James Version except when New International Version (NIV) is indicated.

Library of Congress Catalog No. 79-67440
ISBN: 0-87239-382-8

Printed in U.S.A.   1980

Dedication

To Herbert and Helen Baynes,
my father and mother,
whose instruction and example inspired
me to worship;
and to Mary Burtschi,
my high-school English teacher,
whose encouragement and love of literature
inspired me to write.

Table of Contents

chapter one

Apologies to Dr. Harris

(The Divine/Human Transaction)

Psalm 116:12-19

When *I'm OK—You're OK* was published a few years back, Thomas A. Harris, M.D., introduced to millions of readers the concept of *transactional analysis.* The book promptly became a best-seller as people became more "OK" than they had ever been before. When understood and applied to everyday communications, the principles and techniques described by Dr. Harris changed countless lives and relationships. People were able to communicate better when they understood their feelings and the feelings of others.

At the risk of oversimplifying the theory, note that *transactional analysis* (TA) is the examination and understanding of all interpersonal communications in light of how the communicators feel about themselves and about each other. Dr. Harris maintains that all of your important relationships are "strongly influenced" by your own self-concept (OK or not OK) and by what you think of everyone else (again, OK or not OK).

One key to unlocking the mysteries of TA is the PAC

principle. PAC (not to be confused with CPA!) stands for the concept that in each of us resides a **Parent,** an **Adult,** and a **Child.** Each time you open your mouth to say something, you enter into a verbal transaction as one of the three yous: **P**arent, **A**dult, or **C**hild. What you say will depend upon your self-image at the moment, and upon your attitude toward the person to whom you are speaking.

Basically, when you speak as Parent, you assume the attitude of superiority (I'm OK; you're not OK). If you feel inferior, or threatened by the transaction, the Child in you will speak (I'm not OK; you're OK). The ideal transaction is completed, of course, by psychologically and emotionally secure individuals who converse as Adults (I'm OK; you're OK). There are a number of combination possibilities, all of which are explored and explained by Dr. Harris, but this nutshell condensation will suffice for our purposes.

Another fundamental principle important to understanding TA is the *stimulus/response* idea. Every conversation (all conversations are transactions, but not all transactions are conversations) includes stimuli and responses. One person initiates a transaction with a stimulus: "It is raining today." Another person makes a response: "The weatherman predicts it will clear before the weekend." Both communicators here are speaking as *Adults,* from the *I'm OK; you're OK* standpoint. Neither feels superior to the other, and neither feels inferior.

If the stimulus is, "It is raining today; you should carry your umbrella," the speaker has assumed the Parent role in the transaction. The response may be, "I don't care if it is raining; I hate carrying an umbrella, and I refuse to do so!" The second communicator is allowing the *Child* in him to speak.

When such a transaction is illustrated, it looks like the following diagram.

8

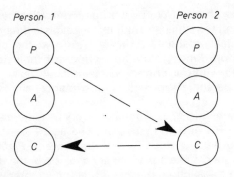

Person 1   Person 2

When Person 1 begins making sounds like a Parent, the stimulus "hooks" the Child in Person 2. That is why the response is a childlike retort. The underlying message of Person 1 is: "I'm OK; you're not OK" ("I must tell you to carry an umbrella, for you haven't the sense to come in out of the rain"). The analyzed response of Person 2 is actually, "I'm not OK, you're not OK" ("I may not be smart enough to carry an umbrella, but you certainly have no right to tell me what to do").

This response of Person 2's Child may very well "hook" the Child of Person 1, so he says, "Oh yeah? And your mother wears army boots!" On the other hand, Person 1 may counter with more communication from his Parent: "Now you know every time you leave your umbrella home on a cloudy day you come home soaking wet!" Etc., etc., etc. You have heard of many such transactions.

Limited space will not allow us to examine all the possible stimuli and responses, nor does the present application require comprehensive analysis of strictly human transactions. This brief introduction to the concepts of TA and PAC will suffice.

The point we're getting to is this: Christian worship is a divine/human transaction, involving stimuli, responses, and counter-responses.

Think about it! Worship is communication between man and God. It is an attitude, an action, a dialogue, a reciprocal relationship. What we do at the church house on Sunday morning, and at our family altars, and alone in our prayer closets, is all in response to God's person, His power, His providence, and His patience.

In terms of TA, God initiates every worship transaction by His gifts to man, bestowed as a *Parent.* That isn't surprising, since God is our Heavenly *Father.*

Now let's make a preliminary analysis of the divine/ human transaction. (Each succeeding chapter will be a more detailed analysis of one communicative exchange that occurs in Christian worship.) By creation, God gives *life* to humans and to parts of their environment. When we acknowledge life as a gift from God, we are prompted to respond to Him with thoughts and acts of worship. We are moved to honor Him, to glorify Him, to trust and obey Him. When God receives genuine worship, He *counter-responds* with more gifts and spiritual blessings, including life everlasting. To make it clear, we may picture the transaction this way:

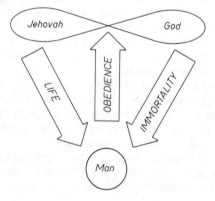

Can you identify the *stimulus,* the *response,* and the *counter-response* in this transaction? Obedience, of course, is worship at its practical best. More than once in the Scriptures God insists that obedience is much to be preferred over empty ceremonial forms that are mere tokens of a superficial piety. (See 1 Samuel 15:22.) God's requirements for citizenship in His kingdom have never changed: trust and obey—there's no other way.

Are you beginning to see the pattern? God gives (stimulus), man worships (response), and God gives again (counter-response). Actually this exchange continues *ad infinitum.* God keeps giving and Christians keep worshiping; God acts and man *re*acts, back and forth, again and again. Faithful worshipers know they can't outgive God. "If ye then, being evil, know how to give good gifts unto your children, how much more shall your Father which is in heaven give good things to them that ask him?" (Matthew 7:11).

The Old Testament hymn writers understood and beautifully expressed the spirit and function of worship. Read these references and let them speak to you: Psalm 116:12-19; Psalm 103; Psalm 107; Psalm 29; and Psalm 84.

The thrust of these passages, and many others, is this: God is great; God is good; I will render worship unto Him for all the benefits He has bestowed upon me and mine. God is worthy to be praised, for He has made us, protected us, delivered us, etc., etc., etc.

David's personal worship was spontaneous. His psalms of praise flowed from a grateful heart. He needed no printed bulletin, no robed choir, and no emcee to cue him as to when he should stand, kneel, sit, or say amen. David prayed, sang, strummed his harp, and composed poems of praise as he was prompted to do so by the revelation of God's power, wisdom, and grace. He even "danced before the Lord" on occasion. All this was inspired response to the greatness and goodness of God and His gifts.

Now, before you jump to the conclusion that you have found a preacher who is opposed to all the structure and forms of late twentieth-century worship—you haven't. You *have* found a preacher, however, who is deeply concerned about modern worshipers who merely go through the motions of worship, or worse, watch from the back pews while others worship. Most to be pitied are those who "worship" at the *electronic church*—they are really only spectators, several thousand watts removed from any genuine Christian body-life.

I am concerned about casual attenders at worship who demonstrate little reverence or humility. I worry about Christians who never "make a joyful noise unto the Lord"; at the same time, I wonder about those who sing every hymn with gusto while daydreaming about last night's entertainment or anticipating Sunday dinner. Even more of a worry are those who "take Communion" without discerning the body and blood of our Lord. Then there are those who share regularly in the fellowship of giving—from the leftover change in their pockets. Many of those are people whose names are conspicuous by their absence from sign-up sheets for volunteer service.

The purpose of this book is not to tell you what I am *against*. I will try to take a positive approach. I am convinced that all Christians need to look closely at Biblical precepts and precedents of worship. We need to examine traditions, patterns, and habits of worship in light of the teaching and examples God has given us. Perhaps we will discover truth that can free us from the boredom and emptiness of habitual rituals. At least this study will be a reminder of the true nature and purpose of Christian worship, which can revitalize our weekly observances and daily devotions.

With apologies then to Dr. Harris, if any are really necessary, the proposition of this work is that Christian worship is a divine/human transaction, stimulated by God and His gifts, rendered by man in attitudes and actions, and answered by God with rich rewards for those who diligently seek Him.

In each subsequent chapter we will analyze one phase of this many-faceted transaction. The chart that follows diagrams the entire analysis as I intend to pursue it.

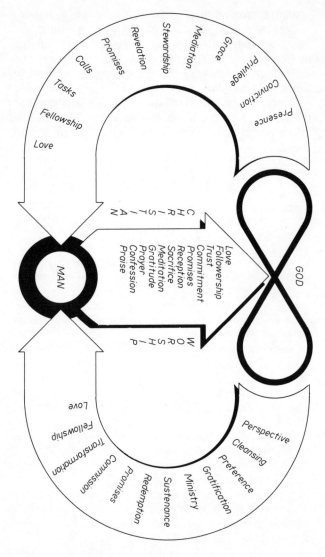

Grace
Privilege
Conviction
Presence

Mediation
Stewardship
Revelation
Promises
Calls
Tasks
Fellowship
Love

MAN

C
H
R
I
S
T
I
A
N

Love
Followership
Trust
Commitment
Promises
Reception
Sacrifice
Meditation
Gratitude
Prayer
Confession
Praise

W
O
R
S
H
I
P

GOD

Love
Fellowship
Transformation
Commission
Promises
Redemption
Sustenance
Ministry
Gratification
Preference
Cleansing
Perspective

14

chapter two

God Really Is OK!

(Presence—Praise—Perspective)

Exodus 3:1-10

No one reading this book will seriously deny that God is OK. Even people who have never made any kind of commitment to God would nevertheless acknowledge His OKness. After all, a "Supreme Being" is *supreme;* a "Super Force" is *super.* There is no way to avoid the greatness of God.

Authentic worship must begin with this premise. God is OK: not merely as OK as our parents, or as our preacher, or as the President. God must be recognized as *super* OK, *supremely* OK, *transcendently* OK. We worship God because He is more OK than anybody, being, or creature in existence. If He is "worthy to be praised" (Psalm 18:3; Revelation 4:11; 5:12) He must be seen as "high and lifted up" (Isaiah 6:1).

True worship is characterized by awe and wonder and adoration. God's majesty inspires awe. God's wisdom fills us with wonder. His presence evokes heartfelt adoration. Whatever we do in worship is ideally motivated by strong convictions about the royalty of God and the thrill of His presence.

This is where the worship transaction begins—with the presence of God. And Christian worship is unique in this regard. Jehovah God dwells in unapproachable light (1 Timothy 6:16), but He himself is not some unapproachable deity who rules us by remote control. He is "the high and lofty One that inhabiteth eternity," but He is "with him also that is of a contrite and humble spirit" (Isaiah 57:15). He is the ruler of the universe, yet He maintains an "open-door policy." He grants unlimited audience to His subjects; we are ushered into His very throne room by the "priesthood of all believers" (1 Peter 2:9). Our God is *accessible,* and so we "come before his presence with singing . . . and into his courts with praise" (Psalm 100).

As the transaction develops, praise is the response of the worshiper to the stimulus of God's presence. Here we must take a critical look at some trends of public worship that have become all too popular and prevalent in our generation. These trends have a common cause—the philosophy of subjectivism so eagerly embraced by the modern masses.

In the name of *informality* God has been insulted and ignored. Worshipers have become casual about their attendance upon the weekly assembly. Even those who are regularly present are careless in dress, posture, conversation, and participation. Their whole bearing and attitude fails to express reverence. The gathering smacks more of social fraternity than of honor and praise rendered to the Lord of lords.

Joe Christian of the 1980's sleeps late on Sunday morning. He arises just in time to throw on a leisure suit, dunk a donut, and speed to the church house. He breathlessly grabs a bulletin at the door, slaps the ushers on the back with loud greetings, and slips into one of the back pews just as the organ begins playing a schmaltzy arrangement of "He Touched Me." He leans forward to discuss the pennant race or the NFL standings with a friend, until he realizes that everyone else is standing to sing the Doxlogy. (He never could understand why they sing that song every Sunday anyway! It must be ancient!)

The toothy emcee badgers the congregation until they say "Good morning" in loud unison. The "song service" includes such all-time favorites as "Happiness Is the Lord" and "I Just Feel Like Something Good Is Going to Happen." Announcement time is light and lively with generous portions of good-natured jest and plenty of "y'all come." "Holy, Holy, Holy" has no place in this program.

Joe Christian tosses his "token" into the offering plate with almost as much thought as he gives to paying a toll on the interstate. Perhaps a little more reverence is demonstrated at Communion time, but he is typically too distracted or preoccupied to concentrate upon the cross.

Joe is always glad when the "preliminaries" are over and it's time for the sermon. Dr. Halefellow Wellmet always has something new, amusing, or clever to say. And he's so "down-home and folksy"! Why, his sermons are so interesting, hardly anybody realizes fifteen minutes have gone by when he's finished.

The "afterglow fellowship" is another favorite part of Sunday for Joe Christian. This is the only time he sees some of his friends, and it's really good to catch up on the news and share a few laughs. Of course the afterglow is preempted sometimes when a convert is baptized at the close of the "service." But that doesn't happen very often.

When "church" is finally over, Joe Christian usually feels *really OK*. He has been with friends, sung some moving songs, sensed a fraternal spirit, been affirmed from the pulpit—and he is proud that he has not spoiled his perfect attendance record.

But what about God? What does Joe think about God? As a matter of fact, has he thought about God at all?

One trouble with modern worship is its almost exclusive emphasis upon the *worshiper* rather than upon the one being worshiped. Christians must restore the objective nature of authentic worship if God is to be honored.

We can begin by singing more *hymns* in place of some of the gospel songs and camp choruses. Try selecting songs with no first-person pronouns (I, me, etc.). Even that may prove difficult, since compilers of church hymnals have also capitulated to the subjective tastes of "jet-set" churchgoers.

Objective worship will include hymns of praise to God, readings from the Word of God, prayers of penitence and petition to God, meditation upon the goodness and greatness of God, exhortation in a message from God, sacrificial offerings to the work of God, and commitment in response to the call of God. The point is that *worship,* if it is worship at all, *is directed toward God.*

Our illustration about Joe Christian may be a bit overdrawn, purposely exaggerated to dramatize the truth. But it is sad to realize how closely that story describes the subjective, shallow, superficial "worship" experience of thousands every Sunday morning. The "fine art of worship," as Andrew Blackwood calls it, has been popularized, secularized, cheapened, and degraded.

"But worship gives me a real good feeling just like it is," someone objects. Who ever told you that the purpose of worship is to make worshipers *feel good?* That kind of subjectivism doesn't come from Scripture. As a matter of fact, true worship will frequently produce quite the opposite effect. But we will deal with that in the next chapter.

Right now, consider the worship experience of Moses in Midian. You will find the record in Exodus 3.

It is important to note what happened when Moses approached the bush that was aflame yet not consumed. God instructed him to remove his shoes because he was on "holy ground." There is no reason to believe that the desert sand surrounding the burning bush was diamond dust or some other precious material. The spot was made sacred only by the presence of God.

Christians are on "holy ground" in the weekly worship assembly, because where even two or three are gathered in the name of Christ, He is in the midst (Matthew 18:20). The bricks and mortar, pulpit and pews are not sacred, any more than the sand and bush of Midian. But wherever God the Father and Jesus the Son are present in the special sense implied by their promises, we must respond to that presence by figuratively taking off our shoes in reverent, worshipful praise.

Can you see how proper worship comes from a proper *perspective?* You have surely heard the anecdote about the tourist in Washington, D.C., who telephoned the minister of the church where the President often worshiped. The tourist wanted to know if the President was expected to attend worship there that Sunday. "That I don't know for certain," replied the minister, "but I can tell you that we are expecting *God* to be here, and we hope His presence will attract a sizeable crowd."

An amusing story, but can you deny that you too would be impressed, even a bit awed, by the presence of the President (even governor or mayor) where you worship? Why don't Christians become more excited about coming into the presence of Jehovah God, Creator, Ruler of the universe, the God of Abraham, Isaac, and Jacob? Think of it! We are privileged to have an audience with the King of all creation. We can enter His palace, kneel at His throne, speak our humble praise, and receive His divine blessing.

That, my friends, should bring spontaneous hosannas from our hearts and lips. "O Worship the King!" "Crown Him With Many Crowns!" "Praise God From Whom All Blessings Flow!" "Blessed Be the Name of the Lord!"

Can we somehow recapture the vision of Isaiah? He saw "the Lord sitting upon a throne, high and lifted up" (Isaiah 6:1). Is your perception of the unseen still intact after the onslaught of realism we all have suffered in this century? Or has your dependence upon sensual stimuli become so ingrown that you are no longer sensitive to divine inspiration? Have you been spiritually de-programmed? Many modern worshipers seem to be saying that the objective view of God "does not compute."

The fact is, of course, that you *do* possess, despite cultural forces and social pressures, a spiritual dimension. You *are* capable of glimpsing God's truth. You *can* become sensitive to the presence of God. The "still small voice" can still be heard by those who filter out the noise of "earthquake, wind, and fire" (1 Kings 19:11, 12).

The Old Testament priests made elaborate preparations and performed all sorts of ceremonies and rituals when they conducted worship before the Lord God of Israel. This was true especially of the high priest, who entered the Holy of Holies on the annual Day of Atonement (Leviticus 16). Ceremonial bathing and formal clothing were required. Detailed instructions were carried out to the letter. Meticulously structured worship in those days was God-ordained, God-centered, and God-visited.

The New Testament church was, for a while, partly (in some places, *predominantly)* peopled by Christian

Jews. Hebrew philosophies, if not customs, of worship carried over. Though far less formal and structured (how much ceremony is possible in a catacomb?), first-century worship at its best was praiseful, prayerful, and purposeful. God was present, worshipers responded in praise, and in the process they received and maintained a proper perspective from which to view God, self, life, and destiny. (See Acts 2:42-47; 4:23-35; 20:7-12.)

If nothing else, worship needs to say something positive about God: He really is OK! His OKness never changes. God is as OK today as when He was worshiped by Abel, Noah, Abraham, Moses, and David. Speaking of David—read his psalms and the psalms of other devout men. Sing them, pray them, commit them to memory. You may want to begin with Psalm 100 or Psalm 77 (verses 13-15).

God is the same OK Father as when Peter and John and Paul worshiped Him. Our conviction ought to be the same as theirs. In the words of the seraphs in Isaiah's vision:

Holy, holy, holy is the Lord of hosts:
the whole earth is full of his glory!

Isaiah 6:3

chapter three

Admit It:
You're Not So OK!

(Conviction—Confession—Cleansing)

Luke 18:9-14

Isaiah was no hoodlum. He was not a thief, an adulterer, a swindler, or a liar. He was no drunkard, not an idolater, nor was he a murderer. Isaiah, son of Amoz, was a godly man. His character and life-style were so exemplary, in fact, that Jehovah selected him to be a divine "mouthpiece." He was to bring God's message to Judah and Jerusalem during that period just following the reign of King Uzziah. It was a critical time, a time much in need of God's word.

Despite his moral goodness, however, the prophet Isaiah felt *not so OK* in the presence of God. The record of his vision and call includes his memorable confession: "Woe is me! for I am undone; because I am a man of unclean lips, and I dwell in the midst of a people of unclean lips" (Isaiah 6:5).

In this experience of Isaiah another significant worship transaction is revealed. God gives the stimulus: *conviction* of sin; man responds with *confession* of sin; and God completes the transaction with spiritual *cleansing* from sin.

22

Here is a twist of irony: *conviction* comes from the Comforter. (See John 16:7, 8, where the King James Version's *reprove* is properly replaced by *convict* in more recent translations.) How comforted do you feel when the Spirit gives you keen awareness of your sin and sinfulness? The agony of heartfelt guilt is hardly a favorite choice in ranking spiritual pleasures. Yet Christian worship is so designed that disturbed worshipers can be comforted, and comfortable worshipers can be disturbed.

It is important to understand that genuine worship will not produce exclusively *good* feelings. Coming into God's presence gives you a humble perspective from which to view not only His greatness and goodness, but also, by marked contrast, your own smallness and unworthiness. If you acknowledge the OKness of God, you must also recognize the uncomfortable truth that you're *not* so OK.

Simon Peter knew that. When Jesus taught His dramatic lesson about fishing and faith, the fisherman was so overwhelmed by humility that he broke into spontaneous worship on the spot. "Depart from me; for I am a sinful man, O Lord" (Luke 5:8). That was some of the finest worshiping Peter ever did. And we can be certain that it pleased Christ, for He later taught in a parable that *humble* worship is the only kind that *justifies* (Luke 18:9-14). *"God be merciful to me a sinner"* is the conviction and the confession prescribed by the Lord for successful worship transactions—worship that results in cleansing for the soul.

But look what has happened to Joe Christian, the average latter-day churchgoer. Our friend Joe has fallen prey to pride. He is proud (some might even say "justly proud") of his ambition and achievements, of his home and family, of his faithfulness and stewardship, of his commitment and loyalty, of his faith and witness. Joe is satisfied, secure, fulfilled, content, and, he thinks, prepared—ready for the Lord's return, or for any intervening contingency.

When Joe Christian hops in his car to drive to the church house, he is filled with the pride of ownership. His house, his automobile, his shoes, his wife and kids—they all bring a special glow of satisfaction. Joe is very pleased with himself. By the time he arrives at the stain-windowed, carpeted, cushioned, chandeliered, air-conditioned church building, he thinks he really *has* arrived. He *looks* fine, he *feels* fine; so he is convinced he *is* fine. His possessions, his health, his satisfaction, his family, and his friends all seem to be saying, "Joe's OK." And Joe has begun to believe it.

"Wait a minute," you object. "Aren't you forgetting the joy of salvation? I know what's happened to Joe. Heaven has come down and glory has filled his soul!"

Very possibly true. But Joe's "I've Got Confidence" needs to be tempered at least occasionally by generous doses of "Only a Sinner Saved by Grace." Jesus taught that the very beginning of blessed happiness is recognition of spiritual poverty (Matthew 5:3).

Can you see the significance of the proper sequence in worship transactions? Before spiritual cleansing can come to the worshiper, he must first become receptive and responsive to the Comforter, God's Holy Spirit. Conviction of sin is not a one-time, pre-baptism, glad-it's-over experience. Personal sin must be acknowledged repeatedly and regularly in the process of conversion, and that process takes a lifetime. As pilgrims progress toward perfection in Christ, their theme song must be, "I Am Not Worthy."

"I am not worthy, this dull tongue repeats it;
I am not worthy, this heart gladly beats it;
Jesus left Heaven to die in my place,
What mercy, what love, and what grace!

Now there is true confession! Your best response to God's stimulus of conviction is *confession.* That is the next order of business in this worship transaction. When you are reminded (convinced) that you're *not so OK,* you need to *admit* it. Not everyone is ready for that; hardly anyone is *always* ready to confess guilt. Therefore guilt too often remains when it could be quickly removed.

Some sinners under conviction resist the Spirit. They never lower their defenses; they will not be moved; they refuse to "let go and let God." These resisters "quench" the Spirit (1 Thessalonians 5:19), throwing cold water and wet blankets on any flame of godly sorrow that threatens to bring them to repentance. Thus they effectively douse the "refiner's fire" (Malachi 3:2).

So there's more than one way to react to spiritual conviction. But *where* and *when* and *how* will Joe Christian respond to God by confession of his sin, if that is indeed his choice? There is no item in the order-of-worship bulletin that announces CONFESSION OF SIN—CONGREGATION WILL KNEEL.

While the Roman church has distorted the doctrine of confession into heresy, many evangelical Christians have largely ignored this vital worship response. When worshipers *do* make a confession to God, it is too often expressed in terms of *sin* in general, rather than *sins* in particular. The average worshiper does not practice the worship of confession.

Perhaps Joe Christian should be issued a sackcloth shift and a pail of ashes as he enters the worship assembly each Sunday. He then would have a reminder, at least, that an essential element of the divine/human transaction is confession of personal sins. Having been provided the accoutrements of repentance, he may muster sufficient humility to admit his imperfections to God.

Facetious suggestions aside, public worship should provide motivations and opportunities conducive to confession. The worship leader may announce, following an appropriate Scripture reading, hymn, or meditation, "Now we shall bow our heads (those who are able to kneel are encouraged to do so) in humble recognition of our sinfulness, and for personal confession of specific sins." A period of silence would follow as each worshiper unburdened his guilty heart before God.

Such confession can (and should) take place at other times, of course, without formal announcement—during the prelude, while offerings are being received, and especially when the Lord's Supper is served. ("Let a man examine himself . . ." 1 Corinthians 11:28.)

Whenever it happens, Joe Christian needs to say to God, "Have mercy, Lord; I am a sinner. I have been too proud to apologize to my wife. I selfishly work overtime for money and promotions at the cost of family togetherness. Sometimes I doubt Your Word, and make excuses for not praying. I have not been giving my employer a full day's work for a day's pay. Forgive me for lusting . . . swearing . . . overeating . . . ignoring needs of others. Have mercy Lord, have mercy!"

This spirit of confession is expressed in J. Edwin Orr's song, *Cleanse Me,* based upon Psalm 139:23.

Search me, O God, and know my heart today;
Try me, O Saviour, know my thoughts, I pray.
See if there be some wicked way in me:
Cleanse me from every sin, and set me free.

We have Biblical assurance that our prayers of confession will be answered. "If we confess our sins, he is faithful and just to forgive us our sins, and to cleanse us from all unrighteousness" (1 John 1:9).

That's how it happened with Isaiah. When he confessed his sinfulness, his uncleanness, his unworthiness—God cleansed his soul. His sin was purged; his iniquity was forgiven. The Heavenly creature applied the purifying fire to Isaiah's "unclean" lips (Isaiah 6:6, 7).

Then the transaction is complete: God counter-responds to man's confession with spiritual *cleansing*. Those who quit reading before they got this far will not know that this is where the *happy* comes in. You see, Heaven *does* come down and fill Joe Christian's soul with glory and confidence—when and *if* he has responded to the Spirit's conviction by humbly confessing his sins. God cleanses penitent confessors from unrighteousness and guilt. This is how the *not OK* worshiper becomes OK.

Job's well-meaning friend, Elihu, reminded the pitiful patriarch of God's faithfulness in this regard: "He looketh upon men, and if any say, I have sinned . . . he will deliver his soul . . . and his life shall see the light" (Job 33:27, 28). In Jesus' parable, the publican who admitted that he was not so OK "went down to his house justified" (Luke 18:14). David underlines the truth from his own experience: "I acknowledged my sin unto thee . . . and thou forgavest the iniquity of my sin" (Psalm 32:5). The classic example of the prodigal son cannot be ignored. To his confession ("I have sinned . . . and am no more worthy to be called thy son") the father responded with joy, gifts, and honor. The wayward sinner was declared "alive" and "found" (Luke 15:18-32). The celebration that followed was festive and fun. But first the prodigal "came to himself" and came to his father confessing his sin.

Spiritual OKness comes to worshipers who repeatedly appropriate Christ's atonement for personal sin. You can understand that. Big words are sometimes needed to express big concepts. But Robert

27

Lowry put it in much simpler terms in the hymn that many of us love to sing with sincere praise and thanksgiving:

> What can wash away my sin?
> What can make me whole again?
> Nothing but the blood of Jesus.

Sinners first contact this saving blood of Jesus in Christian baptism (Romans 6:1-6), "and the blood of Jesus Christ his Son cleanseth us from all sin" (1 John 1:7). We are saved from the guilt of all our past sins with that momentous commitment (1 Peter 3:21). Unfortunately, sinners don't entirely quit sinning when they become Christians. Even the apostle Paul committed unwillful sin (Romans 7:19). Thus the necessity of regularly renewing our repentance, our confession, and our contact with the blood, in partaking the Lord's Supper. (See Matthew 26:26-28.) More about this in Chapter 6. Suffice it here to say that the worship transaction that includes *conviction, confession,* and *cleansing* is a continuing process by which you are becoming what God wants you to be.

chapter four

Your Child Talks to Your Father

(Privilege—Prayer—Preference)

1 Timothy 2:1-8

"I'm My Own Grandpa!" was a popular novelty song of a few years back. It was cute, clever, and intentionally confusing. The title of this chapter is meant to be *clever;* you may even think it's *cute;* but if it *confuses* you, some other title would have been better.

You will recall from the first chapter's discussion of Dr. Harris' PAC principle that every personality is a combination of *Parent, Adult,* and *Child.* In worship transactions with the Heavenly Father, you assume the Child's perspective (I'm not OK; you're OK). Jesus himself introduced that concept when He stressed the childlike nature of kingdom people (Luke 18:17). In a number of New Testament passages, Christians are declared to be "children of God" (e.g. Romans 8:16; Galatians 3:26). Jesus and His earliest followers frequently spoke of God as their "Father" (Matthew 7:21; 10:32; Philippians 4:20, etc.).

That should explain the title above: your *Child* (the child that is a part of your own personality) talks (communicates, prays) to your Father (the *Heavenly*

Father, God). And that title accurately labels and introduces the subject matter of this chapter. The topic is *prayer*—prayer analyzed as a worship transaction, both public and private. Yes, *private* worship is also a consideration in this study, one that has not been stressed until now. A comprehensive consideration of prayer, of course, includes personal, family, and cell-group prayers, as well as prayers in formal, public worship. Spoken prayers, silent prayers, sentence prayers, conversational prayers, flash prayers—the subject is really too broad to cover in detail here. But the brief analysis offered in these few paragraphs is applicable to prayer in general.

Prayer can be used as a synonym for *worship.* Check the chart on page 14 for comparison. The center column of words extending upward from *man* to *God* represents the responses that are central to the divine/human transaction of worship. How many of those words that describe acts of worship also describe what happens in prayer (when prayer is at its best)? Worship, the public kind in particular, simply gives a variety of expressions to that which is called prayer under other circumstances.

God may be praised in song, but many songs are really prayers set to music. Public reading of the Scriptures is usually a part of formal worship, and again, dozens of Bible passages are actually transcripts of prayers offered by children of God through the centuries. Ideally, offerings are given with prayer, the Lord's Supper is received with prayer, and sermons are delivered and audited with prayer. In public worship the prayer thoughts of trust and love and commitment are translated into actions: the giving of tithes and offerings, the taking of Communion emblems, even the stepping forward to declare faith and to become obedient in Christian baptism. Prayer and worship are two sides of the same coin; that coin is *communication with God.* In our praying are we sometimes so engrossed with ourselves, companions, or procedures that we fail to get in touch with Him?

Jane Christian is so busy with prayer disciplines, prayer lists, prayer partners, and prayer meetings that she has forgotten that prayer is a *privilege.* She arises an hour early each morning to keep her "appointment with God." Her prayer list is so long she keeps it on adding-machine tape. She attends weekly meetings of a Kaffee Klatch Prayer Group, the Ladies Aid Prayer Group, the New Mothers Prayer Group, the Deacon's Wives Prayer Group, and the Women-for-Missions Prayer Group. She has become a prayer groupie! The Mid-week Prayer Meeting at the church house and regular rendezvous with her personal prayer partner round out the week.

Our friend Jane is obeying, quite literally, the imperative of Paul to "pray without ceasing" (1 Thessalonians 5:17). She is, however, beginning to show signs of weariness in well-praying. Insufficient sleep has turned her into a grouchy hypochondriac. Her neglected family is ready to mutiny. And worst of all, the privilege of prayer has become to Jane a beastly burden of responsibility.

In case you are at this moment being tempted to use these last paragraphs as some sort of rationale to discontinue whatever you may be doing in the way of regular prayer practices—forget it! (That is, unless you, like Jane, have jumped overboard to keep from missing the boat.) This is not being written to excuse those whose only prayer is table grace, or the midnight mumblers who regularly fall asleep in the middle of their "now-I-lay-me-downs."

The point being made is this: prayer is a *privilege.* God stimulates our prayer life by giving us the opportunity, the possibility, of actually talking to Him. Have you tried to arrange an interview with the President lately? How many kings and queens have granted you an audience? Pick up your phone right now and place a call to the governor of your state. Tell me when you hear his voice—I won't be holding my breath!

Can you see what a gift has been given us? It's the chance of a lifetime. Audrey Mieir said it this way:

Although He has millions of souls to see about;
Although the sun, the moon, and the stars are
    in His care;
How wonderful to know, wherever you may go,
He can be reached just by a whispered prayer!

This is why Christians make prayer a matter of top priority. When one is invited to the throne room, one does not waste the opportunity (as did the pussycat in the nursery rhyme) by giving attention to frolicking rodents. We are foolish to spurn, by neglect and abuse, the privilege of praying.

Anthony Ash, in his study book on prayer, writes, "It is obvious that, if the followers of the Lord are to find the spiritual rejuvenation they so much need, the dynamic of prayer must be rediscovered." G. Campbell Morgan, the famous preacher, said, "There is nothing the church needs more at the present hour than to understand what a real prayer meeting is." Thomas A. Carruth, world prayer leader, further underlines the urgency of prayer: "The last best hope of the human race is in some form of united, world-wide prayer."

The apostle Paul urged the priority of prayer for young Timothy's ministry: "I exhort therefore, that, first of all, supplications, prayers, intercessions, and

32

giving of thanks, be made for all men. . . . For this is good and acceptable in the sight of God our Saviour. . . . I will therefore that men pray every where" (1 Timothy 2:1, 3, 8).

A pattern for private prayer is outlined simply by the acrostic J-O-Y: praise to *Jesus*; intercession for *Others*; and petitions for *Yourself*. These elements will be present in conscientious personal worship.

Jesus emphasized that prayer should be practiced "in secret" (Matthew 6:6). A prayer "closet" may become increasingly necessary in this day of noisy distractions. Someone suggested that secret prayer is like using a telephone booth at night: when you step inside and close the door, the *light* comes on.

Family prayers and public prayers, of course, are not precluded by this teaching of the Lord. His chief concern in this context was *prideful, self-righteous* prayer. One clear instruction He gave pertaining to public worship was, "My house shall be called of all nations the house of prayer" (Mark 11:17). So it is right that our weekly assemblies are marked by several calls to prayer. The Christian worshiper must keep in mind the *purpose* of these various public supplications. They are not structured into the worship program simply to take up space in the bulletin. (It is especially tragic when *leaders* of worship in prayer do not remember the specific purpose of their praying.)

The invocation asks (invokes) God's presence and His blessing upon the proceedings. The offertory prayer expresses thanksgiving to God for material wealth, and asks His blessing upon the tithes and offerings, to the end that His will be "done on earth as it is in heaven." Prayers at the Lord's table concentrate upon remembering Calvary and honoring Christ. A pastoral prayer usually makes petitions on behalf of particular people in special need. Pastors will lead the thinking of the congregation to specific causes and concerns. A prayer just prior to the sermon will ask God's blessing on both the message and messenger. The "benediction" (blessing) once more asks God's watch care upon worshipers, this time as they are dismissed and go their separate ways.

It is neither necessary nor desirable for *every* public prayer to include *every* purpose. Indeed, such a practice can bring about the very worst sort of "vain repetitions" (Matthew 6:7).

By virtue of the specific purpose of public prayers, they should be mostly brief. Whether they are long or short, however, individual worshipers must participate by listening carefully and/or by thinking personal prayers of a similar nature as the leader prays aloud.

When Christians respond to God's gift of privilege in prayer, God counter-responds with *preferential* treatment. "The effectual fervent prayer of a righteous man availeth much" (James 5:16). "And all things, whatsoever ye shall ask in prayer, believing, ye shall receive" (Matthew 21:22). "If my people . . . shall humble themselves, and pray . . . then will I hear from heaven, and will forgive their sin, and will heal their land" (2 Chronicles 7:14). The transaction is thus once more completed by God, and worshipers' faith in the power of prayer is reconfirmed.

If God's answers to prayer are not always according to *our* will, we may reconcile ourselves to disappointments or postponements by recalling the truth expressed so well by George Buttrick: "Prayer is not an easy way of getting what we want, but the only way of becoming what God wants us to be."

Let me share with you three prayers I cannot forget. Roy Weece, campus minister at the University of Missouri, tells of a student who was overheard praying beside his bed with an open Bible before him. He said, "Lord, I know this is true; help me to believe it." Such a prayer expresses an honest struggle for faith.

34

Another meaningful prayer was offered at a North American Christian Convention several years ago. The gentleman on the platform concluded with this: "Father, grant these petitions, not because we are perfect, or even good—but because we *want* to be so very much." We all need to communicate to God our humble hunger for righteousness.

In a school play, *The Curious Savage,* Fairy Mae, a resident in a home for the mentally disturbed, kneels in front of a keyhole in the parlor door to see who has come into the front hall. She is advised by another resident that one should kneel only to pray. Fairy Mae's rejoinder is, "Then I'll say a prayer—Dear Lord, let me see something!" That prayer is at once amusing and poignant. All Christians should regularly petition God for personal spiritual vision—to see Him, His work, and our own abilities and opportunities more clearly.

chapter five

Your Maturing Child Says Thank You

(Grace—Gratitude—Gratification)

Psalm 32

This chapter was at first entitled: *"Where's Your Thanksgiving, Turkey?"* Cute, eh? But it seems flip, even fraudulent, considering the serious theme of this section. Thanksgiving is the worship response to be analyzed here, but the transaction begins with God's gift of grace.

Your children, the offspring of your marriage, should, of course, learn early to say "Thank you." But proper child rearing is not a primary concern of this study. Remember that in TA terminology, your *Child* is that part of your triune personality (PAC) that is "hooked" by the stimuli of gifts from Father God. The discussion being introduced here is an analysis of the transaction of worship in which you as a grateful *Child* express sincere thanks to a gracious Heavenly *Parent.*

You may be tempted to challenge the analogy at this point. You may want to object that once a sinner has received God's grace, he can assume the *I'm OK— You're OK* position in worship transactions. Your point is well taken, and there is indeed a weakness in the application of the PAC principle here, due to the fact that Dr. Harris designed TA for human/human relationships. Divine/human transactions are really beyond the scope of the theory in some respects.

The Bible teaches, however, that when God's grace is received "through faith" (Ephesians 2:8), we become "the children of God" (Galatians 3:26). We are adopted into His great family, and become "joint-heirs with Christ" (Romans 8:15-17). So our approach to God remains *I'm not OK—You're OK,* for we are *children* of the Father, *sinners* saved only by grace. The most we can say in analyzing the PAC of Christians is that their Child is *maturing.*

Your next question may be, "Is gratitude a typical child's response?" Here again the analogy falls a bit short. Grateful children are *made,* not born. The raw instincts of human (carnal) nature do not lean to thanksgiving. Gratitude is a *learned* response. Young children must be taught to say "Thank you"—and even when they say the words, they may rarely *feel* thankful. (It is important, by the way, for them and us to express thanks whether we feel like it or not.)

But spiritual children of God are *adults* in other realms. Your conscience has been educated, and your responses have been trained by experience. And as you continue to grow in Christ you will become more and more programmed for gratitude. Your *Child* will mature—yet your position before God will forever remain inferior. Even the *desire* for equality with the Father is sin. (Consider Eve, Genesis 3:4-6, and Lucifer, Isaiah 14:12-15.)

More later about the gratitude attitude. The first step in analyzing this segment of the worship transaction is to recognize the stimulus of God's gift of grace. Volumes have already been written about divine grace, and only gross presumption would suppose that this brief study will offer any new light. One or two aspects of the topic will be examined here to reconfirm what you may already know.

If you have read any of the aforementioned volumes, you understand that grace is *undeserved favor.* Sinners are offered forgiveness and adoption as sons, not because they deserve such gifts, but because they *need* to be forgiven and adopted. Joe and Jane Christian are apt to feel that personal redemption is a "certain inalienable right"—until they come to grips with their own need for saving grace. God "looks beyond our fault and sees our need."

Speaking of *need,* have you ever suspected that your "conversion experience" is somehow second-rate because you never *needed* it as badly as some converts do? When you have heard and read a few Christian testimonies from people who have been rescued from the very dregs of despicable and diabolical iniquity you can develop a pretty good inferiority complex over your own sparse crop of wild oats. Ironic, isn't it, that you can actually feel discontented, even *guilty,* because you were never an alcoholic, a prostitute, or a drug addict? It is a real problem though, because Christians who are not sure they were ever *lost* can hardly be certain that they are saved. Others who don't actually doubt their salvation still envy the sense of relief, release, freedom, and joy possessed by those who have "truly been lifted from the miry clay."

Case in point: me. I was just eight years old when I publicly declared my faith in Christ and was baptized "for remission of sins." The problem is that my most serious transgression up to that moment had been disregarding the bell that signaled the end of a kindergarten recess period.

(Fact of the matter is, I was too busy chasing a pretty little girl around the school playground even to *hear* the bell. We were both promptly punished by swats with a ruler across the back of our hands. You may be interested to know that my own mother was the teacher, and this was the only corporal punishment I suffered in my entire educational career!)

My folks and friends may remember other infractions, but at that age I was basically a good boy. I was born to thoroughly Christian parents, and they trained me in "the way I should go;" in the "nurture and admonition of the Lord."

Allow me a paragraph in praise of my godly parents. Their conviction and commitment to the cause of Christ is without flaw. They have sacrificed to serve Jesus unselfishly from the day they simultaneously surrendered to His call. Their life-style has been beyond reproach; their behavior always exemplary. We children (there are five of us) were good, and became Christians, not because we were reared in a preacher's home (yes, we're PK's), but because we were reared in a Christian home. If the Lord is willing, Herbert and Helen Baynes will celebrate their golden wedding anniversary this summer. Their children will "rise up and call them blessed," and they will continue to give all the glory to God.

But you can see why I was concerned during one period of my life that my conversion simply was not dramatic enough. My decision was made with tears, and with as much heartfelt sincerity as an eight-year-old can muster. I recall being released from the fear of a destiny in Hell without Christ. But as the years went by, my spiritual gratitude somehow faded as I reflected on the nature of my personal pilgrimage. Finding your way home is no big deal if you've only been at the next-door neighbor's. Coming home spiritually may not seem that significant when you've never wandered far from God. These doubts and frustrations were further compounded by guilt when I found myself sinning more as a Christian than I ever had before my decision. I wrestled with all of this for too long until I finally created an illustration that satisfies my mind.

Young parents of two fine boys moved to a country place bordered at the back by a flood canal. The canal was cut deep, creating a sharp cliff just beyond the property line. A fence was promptly erected, and the boys, of course, were warned not to play near the gorge.

One spring afternoon, however, these small boys climbed the fence so they could throw stones in the canal. The water was at "high tide" due to winter thaw and early rains. Absorbed in the fun of their play, they moved closer and closer to the cliff's edge. As he threw a large rock, the older brother lost his footing and fell twenty feet into the cold, swift current of the drainage canal.

The boys' father had come home from work in the meantime, and missed the usual hearty greetings from his sons. Where could those rascals be? He checked the back yard, then on instinct walked all the way to the fence. He spotted his younger son at the same time he heard the scream of panic. Vaulting the fence, he ran to the cliff where the small boy stood precariously close to the edge. The frightened child was leaning over the chasm shouting to his brother, who was bobbing swiftly out of earshot.

At once the father snatched his younger son back from cliff's edge, ran to the fence, and lifted him over. "Run and tell Mom to call the rescue squad," he yelled. "I'm going to help your brother." With that he leaped back to the canal, kicked off his shoes, and dived over the side.

Superhuman swimming in the fast current brought him quickly to his son, now frantic with fear. Man and boy managed somehow to struggle to the perpendicular side of the ditch. There they clung desperately to

40

exposed roots until help came. Minutes later they were lifted to safety.

Do you see the truth of this modern parable? Just as surely as this loving father saved his older son from drowning, he saved the younger son too. Though I may have been only on the brink of sin and damnation at age eight, my Heavenly Father is saving me just as surely as if He had rescued me from the very depths of degradation. He is saving me from canals of sin and guilt into which I have never fallen, for He has lifted me to safety. "He hideth my soul in the cleft of the rock."

My conversion is just as real, just as dramatic, just as miraculous as anyone's. I am being saved from sins I *have not* committed as well as from sins I *have* committed. I am saved and safe in Jesus. And you are too, if you are trusting and obeying Him. That is what makes us grateful for God's grace. When we express our gratitude, it becomes worship. Webster says that *thanksgiving* is "a celebration of divine goodness."

The extent of our celebration and the quality of our gratitude are determined by our attitude toward God's forgiveness. Simon, a Pharisee who entertained Jesus in his home, criticized the Master for accepting the humble worship of an uninvited guest, a "sinful woman." The Lord rebuked Simon with a frank lesson about forgiveness, self-righteousness, love, and hospitality. He said, in essence, "This woman acknowledges her great sinfulness, thus her grateful response to forgiveness. Her love for me is great. But since you will not admit the sins for which you need forgiveness, your love (gratitude) is little." (See Luke 7:36-48).

Since we are saved from *all* sin and unrighteousness (1 John 1:9), our response to God's grace knows no bounds. Limitless gratitude flows forth in thankful praise:

A wonderful Savior is Jesus my Lord . . .

He hideth my life in the depths of His love,
And covers me there with His hand.

A more recent musical expression of worshipful gratitude is Andraé Crouch's *My Tribute* (To God Be the Glory):

How can I say thanks for the things
  You have done for me?
Things so undeserved, yet You give to prove
  Your love for me.
The voices of a million angels could not
  express my gratitude;
All that I am and ever hope to be,
  I owe it all to Thee.[1]

Spiritual gratification comes to the worshiper as this transaction is completed: peace "which passeth all understanding" (Philippians 4:7). God multiplies and compounds the spiritual pleasures of forgiven sinners as He receives our thanks and accepts our worship.
David exhorts us in his psalm of gratitude:

Blessed is he whose transgression is forgiven, whose sin is covered. . . . Be glad in the Lord, and rejoice, ye righteous: and shout for joy, all ye that are upright in heart (Psalm 32:1, 11).

Paul underlines the thought in his letter to Christians at Colossae:

And let the peace of God rule in your hearts, to the which also ye are called in one body; and be ye thankful. Let the word of Christ dwell in you richly in all wisdom; teaching and admonishing one another in psalms and hymns and spiritual songs, singing with grace in your hearts to the Lord. And whatsoever ye do in word or deed, do all in the name of the Lord Jesus, giving thanks to God and the Father by him (Colossians 3:15-17).

chapter six

Your Child's Treasury of Memories

(Mediation—Meditation—Ministry)

1 Corinthians 11:23-29

Joe and Jane Christian have exceptional forgetters. It's not that they forget to pay their health insurance premiums, or to change the oil in their cars, or to have their annual furnace checkup. They usually remember birthday and anniversary dates, social security numbers, and even PTA meetings. They rarely miss a dentist appointment, always return library books on time, and have only failed once or twice to set the garbage out on Tuesday.

The Christians' memory lapse occurs, tragically enough, in the *spiritual* realm. They forget that Christ died on a cross at Calvary. Oh, the historical fact itself has not escaped recall. But the divine purpose and personal implications of Jesus' death rarely come to mind during the average workday, or while Joe and Jane are water skiing on the weekend.

Jesus knew His disciples had good forgetters. That's why He instituted the memorial feast, which we call the *Lord's Supper,* prior to His crucifixion. "This do in remembrance of me," He said (Luke 22:19).

Christ provided a reminder by ordaining the worship-ful observance of "Communion." The first-century church was faithful in "the breaking of bread" (Acts 2:42), partaking at least weekly (Acts 20:7), perhaps more often. Ard Hoven maintains that the "supper is a deliberate attempt by our Lord to stir our hearts and minds and cause us to keep remembering that which was done for us at Calvary" *(Meditations and Prayers for the Lord's Table,* Standard Publishing, 1963).

> Lest I forget Gethsemane;
> Lest I forget Thine agony;
> Lest I forget Thy love for me
> Lead me to Calvary.
> —Jennie E. Hussey

Monuments, holidays, ceremonies, flags, songs, pictures—we are surrounded by memorials of all kinds. We must admit that we need reminders even of those people, events, and ideals that are most impor-tant to us. It has always been that way.

Israel was given Passover to help them remember their divine deliverance from Egyptian slavery (Exodus 12:21-27). They were given the ark of the covenant to remind them of God's providence for them during the years of wandering (Hebrews 9:1-5). The ark con-tained a pot of manna to memorialize the miraculous feeding of Israel in the wilderness (Exodus 16:31-35). There was also Aaron's rod that budded when God chose him and his to be the tribe of priests (Numbers 17:8-10). The third memorial in the ark was the "tes-timony" and law of God, the Ten Commandments en-graved on tablets of stone (Deuteronomy 10:3-5).

45

When God's children finally crossed Jordan to enter the promised land, twelve stones were taken from the middle of the river "for a memorial unto the children of Israel for ever" (Joshua 4:1-7).

Time after time God gave His people something to think about. It was, and is, important for them, and us, to reminisce concerning God's power, His justice, His compassion, and His activity in human affairs. It is essential (indeed, *commanded)* that memories of God's goodness and greatness be shared by each generation with the next (Psalm 145:4-7). This same intergenerational perpetuation of faith was commended by Paul to Timothy for evangelism (2 Timothy 2:2). (The effectiveness of this relay method of education has been proven by Frank Laubach's "each-one-teach-one" strategy for world literacy.)

But wait! Who sneaked in that cart being pushed by a horse? That part of the worship transaction will be analyzed a few pages later.

The stimulus for worship at the Lord's table is God's gift of *mediation* through Christ (1 Timothy 2:5). Because sinners are *not OK* with God, we need a "go-between" to plead our case and our cause before Him (Hebrews 9:15; 1 John 2:1, 2). When Joe and Jane and you and I partake of the sacred loaf and cup, it is in response to God's perfect solution to the justice/mercy dilemma.

God's universal law has always been this: "The soul that sinneth, it shall die" (Ezekiel 18:4). The New Testament underscores that unchanging truth: "The wages of sin is death" (Romans 6:23). It is clear that God's justice requires a death penalty for sin. Since all have sinned (Romans 3:23), all mankind is sentenced to death. Here is where the dilemma develops, for "The Lord is . . . not willing that any should perish" (2 Peter 3:9). Divine *mercy* is diametrically opposed to the doom imposed by divine *justice.*

Frank Bush, in his *Prospectus for Evangelism,* illustrates the dilemma and its solution in the drawing reprinted below. The substitionary death of Christ on the cross at once satisfied the justice of God and expressed the mercy of God. There is God's gift of mediation.

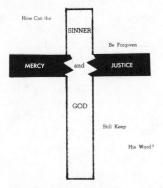

Jesus paid it all,
All to Him I owe;
Sin had left a crimson stain,
He washed it white as snow.
—Elvina M. Hall

Now, *that* is what Joe and Jane Christian need to think about at "Communion time." They will have to consciously concentrate *(meditate)* on such thoughts, for distractions abound. Crying babies, whispering juveniles, note-passing teens, stumbling deacons, bulletin-shuffling visitors, and snoring senior citizens may divert their attention. The organ music, bright sun through stained glass, traffic noise, neighborhood lawn mowers, or the preacher's too-short socks can interrupt their train of thought. Their minds begin to wander, and shortly they realize with consternation that everyone has been served, and Joe and Jane have

47

eaten and drunk damnation unto themselves, "not discerning the Lord's body" (1 Corinthians 11:29). So they flash a quick prayer, "God, forgive me my careless meditation," and immediately become absorbed in the special music, the sermon, or the announcements.

Communion meditation must be transcendental—that is, your thought must be concentrated upon spiritual truths rather than upon material distractions. The typical worshiper of today is inexperienced in prolonged meditation upon the transcendent. Many in the TV generation have surrendered their thinking capacity to the "mind benders" of the commercial entertainment industry. Some are actually frightened when they find themselves alone with their thoughts. They reach for the television knob, the radio switch, or the CB tuner, to find either mere distraction or someone who will *tell* them what to think. In desperation they may even grab a book or magazine to occupy their minds. But one thing is clear, they don't want to *think*. Thought requires effort and energy; it often produces guilt or other mental pain; it may even challenge to positive action, and shake the thinker out of apathy. Thinking is not easy, but it is *right*.

Christians must be thinkers. Some of our deepest thoughts will come to us in communion with Christ, as we contemplate the miracle of mediation. Jesus knew we would often feel far removed by time and distance from the realities of Calvary. He instituted the memorial of His supper to bridge those mental gaps, to refresh our memories of the Master and of His ministry to our personal spiritual needs.

Here are some practical ideas to help you meditate properly in Communion:

1. **Close your eyes and ears; open your mind.** Shut out distractions, and listen for the "still small voice" of God.

2. **Picture Calvary.** Create a mental image of Golgotha, the crosses, the soldiers, the thieves. Zoom in for a closeup of Jesus, the thorns, the nails, and the spear wound. Put yourself in the crowd at the foot of the cross. What are you thinking, saying, doing?

3. **Identify with Christ's suffering.** Put yourself in His place; walk in His shoes; look through His window. Can you feel the physical pain? the psychological rejection? the spiritual agony?

4. **Define doctrines of salvation.** Phrase explanations of *atonement, reconciliation, propitiation, redemption,* etc. in words your unchurched friends would understand.

5. **Quote pertinent Scriptures.** Make it a discipline of your daily devotions to memorize Bible verses that speak of Christ's death for sinners (John 3:16; Romans 5:6-8; Philippians 2:5-11; etc.) Silently recite them at Communion time.

6. **Reconstruct the crime.** Rehearse in your mind the events just preceding the crucifixion; try to recall as many details as possible.

7. **Listen to Jesus.** Mentally list the "seven sayings of the cross."

8. **Be a disciple.** Imagine you are Peter, Thomas, John, or one of the two on the road to Emmaus. Role-play their experiences in your mind. Project yourself into their reactions to the crucifixion.

Peter Marshall gives us all something to think about in his sermon, "Were You There?"

They were all there that day on the top of the hill—the friends of Jesus and His enemies. The church people, they were there, as well as the people who never went to church . . . and the people who were always talking about the church and always talking about the Lord, the pious people on whose lips there were always glib quotations from the Scriptures—they were there. The unbelievers were standing beside them. . . . When we consider who were there and when we are honest with ourselves, we know that we were there and that we helped to put Christ there. . . . Every human being was represented on Calvary. Every sin was in a nail, or the point of a spear, or the thorns. . . . Calvary still stands. And you and I erect the Cross again and again and again every time we sin. The hammer blows are still echoing somewhere in the caverns of your heart and mine—every time we deny Him—every time we sin against Him or fail to do what He commanded. He is being crucified again and again and again. Were you there when they crucified my Lord? I was—were you?

The pattern of this vital worship transaction is completed as God blesses participants in the supper with *ministry.* Paul said, "As often as ye eat this bread, and drink this cup, ye do show the Lord's death till he come" (1 Corinthians 11:26). The *New International Version* reads *proclaim* rather than *do show.* Eating the Lord's Supper preaches a sermon about His atoning sacrifice. All participating believers who partake worthily are ministers of reconciliation (2 Corinthians 5:18).

It is not as if we were merely talking to *ourselves* about the saving death of Christ (important as it is to exhort one another in Christian fellowship). We proclaim the Lord's death to the unsaved world too, when they understand that this memorial is central to the purpose of our weekly assemblies. The message that we proclaim is more than the *fact* of Jesus' execution and burial. It includes God's plan and purpose in His redemptive sacrifice, and His victory over death, the reason for the hope that is in us (1 Peter 3:15).

chapter seven

What's It Like to Have a Rich Father?

(Stewardship—Sacrifice—Sustenance)

2 Corinthians 8:1-7

Orphan Annie never had it so good! Your OK "Father is rich in houses and lands; He holdeth the wealth of the world in His hands! Of rubies and diamonds, of silver and gold, His coffers are full, He has riches untold."[1]

Being a child of the King, you are entrusted with His wealth and with the gift of *stewardship.* You are a steward of God's estate, a caretaker of His property. All that you possess is owned by God.

The exercise of Christian stewardship is an expression of worship that really embraces all other expressions of worship. God's children become "living sacrifices, holy and pleasing to God—which is your spiritual worship" (Romans 12:1, NIV). Being a faithful steward means far more than contributing generously and cheerfully to the weekly offering received in public assembly. But since wealth, especially in America, is usually thought of, spoken of, and written of in terms of dollars and cents, the discussion of stewardship usually begins with consideration of money.

As a matter of fact, sometimes Joe Christian complains that "all they ever talk about at church is money!" It truly may seem like that to Joe, of course, because he attends public worship only spasmodically, and coincidence (or providence) has more than once made the topic of the lesson or sermon "Stewardship of Treasure." Also to be considered is the defensive attitude Joe has developed about church giving because he gives so little. His guilt from selfishness has so sharpened his sensitivity to the topic that no *hint* of inference or allusion to giving passes his notice. Joe is especially attuned to words and phrases that he suspects are aimed at his wallet.

Actually, it should come as no surprise that a lot of talk about money is heard at public worship. As more than several preachers have pointed out, Jesus himself said more about money than He said about any other single topic, including the important subjects of Heaven and Hell. Howard Hendricks, head of the Department of Christian Education at Dallas Theological Seminary, suggests that Jesus made this emphasis "because money cuts deep into character."

Your character *is* profoundly affected by your attitude toward possessions. How do you feel about what you have? How much more do you want? Is your goal to accumulate wealth? What *is* the purpose of your work? Face it—stewardship, faithful or unfaithful, is what makes you tick!

The Father has given you more than a small allowance. As an adopted son you are "an heir of God through Christ" (Galatians 4:7). You are named in His will! You're in the money—and it's not subject to inheritance tax! You have a rich Father, and He's not a mere Daddy Warbucks.

I'm a child of the King,
A child of the King:

With Jesus my Savior
I'm a child of the King.[1]

That's the good news. What you may consider to be *not* so good news is this: "Unto whomsoever much is given, of him shall be much required" (Luke 12:48). America is a bad place to live if you're not keen on being a faithful Christian steward. Domestic affluence provides riches and luxuries unattainable in other countries, yet American Christians must therefore bear a greater burden of responsibility as caretakers of such wealth. It is a *burden,* that is, to those who have not recognized stewardship as a privilege granted by God.

When you acknowledge that stewardship is a gift from God, your maturing *Child* is "hooked" by the stimulus, and your worship response is *sacrifice.* Whether you "give till it hurts" or "give until it feels good," your Sunday offering is a sacrificial response to stewardship. Truth is, church giving at its best is neither motivated nor evaluated strictly by feelings. And it is important to remember that all "sacrifices" are not necessarily acceptable in God's sight (e.g. Cain—Genesis 4:5).

In its broadest definition, *sacrifice* describes a one-dollar offering as well as a ten-dollar offering. When a worshiper gives any money at all to God's work, he is sacrificing (foregoing) some possession or pleasure that could have been purchased with that amount. Sacrificial giving, however, is generally understood to be an offering that imposes upon the giver deprivation of necessary (according to community standards) provisions.

Since most "community standards" of living in our country are inflated, Joe and Jane Christian may have rather distorted ideas about sacrifice. Distinctions between necessities and luxuries have become blurred.

They may feel deprived if their television is only a black-and-white model, or if they have only one set in the house. They may think it a genuine sacrifice to limit their dining-out to once a month. They can develop sincere martyr complexes if their cars are more than five years old, or if their house has only one bathroom, or if each kid in the family doesn't own a ten-speed bicycle.

When Christians determine to worship God with *sacrifice,* they must evaluate their stewardship in terms of a broader community—the whole community of man. In other words, assess your personal welfare by contrast with the *poorer* persons you know about, rather than with the *richer* people of your acquaintance. How many millions more exist in that first category!

The Christians at Corinth had their problems, but they *could* do something right. They were prompted by the poverty of the saints in Jerusalem to give liberal offerings for a special collection administered by the apostle Paul. Congregations in Galatia and Macedonia were contributing also. Paul instructed them to share in this fellowship of giving at their weekly public assemblies for worship. "On the first day of every week, each one of you should set aside a sum of money in keeping with his income, saving it up, so that when I come no collections will have to be made" (1 Corinthians 16:2, NIV).

Paul was a fund raiser par excellence. He encouraged Corinthians to sacrifice by telling them of the Macedonians' generosity: "They gave as much as they were able, and even beyond their ability" (2 Corinthians 8:3, NIV). He inspired the Macedonians to give by making an example of the Corinthians' enthusiasm: "For I know your eagerness to help, and I have been boasting about it to the Macedonians" (2 Corinthians 9:2, NIV). He further prodded the Corinthians to give

54

their best by reporting to them his boast: "I am sending the brothers in order that our boasting about you in this matter should not prove hollow" (2 Corinthians 9:3, NIV). This spirit of unity and fellowship (even friendly competition?) was exploited to the end that the Jerusalem Christians might have their needs supplied (2 Corinthians 8:14). The genius of this program of finance was that it was reciprocal. Through pure, free-will, non-compulsory sharing, the Christians accomplished what communism falsely promises. Each contributed according to his ability, and each received according to his need.

But the "living sacrifice" that is our "spiritual worship" takes stewardship beyond the passing of the plate. Your money is a valuable asset to God's kingdom, but what about the *rest* of you? "Know ye not that . . . ye are not your own? For ye are bought with a price: therefore glorify God in your body, and in your spirit, which are God's" (1 Corinthians 6:19, 20).

Talents, skills, influence, experience, and time are also gifts entrusted to our care. Good stewards must be "found faithful" in all of these (1 Corinthians 4:2). Think about *time,* for example. I am persuaded that most Christians are more willing these days to give *money* to the Lord's church than they are to give *time.* Another irony of our age is that more leisure time is available than ever before, and yet people seem more stingy with their time-off hours than when they worked dawn-to-dusk six days a week just to eke out a living.

The every-member ministry of the church is a volunteer agency that requires sharing of time by every Christian. As in stewardship of money, you should give time to kingdom causes as you have been prospered. If all the church members who are proud of giving one day in seven "to God" were investing twenty-four hours of every week in Christian service, the Lord's commission could be fulfilled in twenty years!

Figure it out. Even if you spend five hours in public worship and study at the church house each week, and even if you give one hour per day to personal Bible study and prayer, twelve hours would be left for a volunteer career in Christian service. You say you need eight hours of God's day to sleep? The challenge is still valid! If two million professing New Testament Christians dedicated even four hours per week (8,000,000 man-hours) to the evangelistic, educational, and benevolent enterprises of the church—who can accurately predict the impact of such a revolution? (The biggest task in such a development would belong to the equipping ministers whose responsibility would be finding enough work for the volunteers. What an exciting prospect!)[2] Two more thoughts:

1. All that we are and all that we have belongs to God. Every moment and every dollar should accordingly be invested to God's glory. Every ability and opportunity must be wisely used in a way that will honor our Lord. If you desire to worship with your very existence, you will seek to justify every expenditure of time, talent, and treasure in the context of total accountability to the Master. Christians must be faithful in appropriating resources that are kept as well as those that are given away.

2. The worship transaction is completed by God, whose promise through Christ is true: "Seek ye first the kingdom of God, and his righteousness; and all these things shall be added unto you" (Matthew 6:33). Day-to-day sustenance is the counter-response of God to worship that is expressed by your living sacrifice. It was so among worshipers under the old covenant (Malachi 3:10), and it is so in the New Testament church (Philippians 4:19). Having a rich Father gives us the confidence to say, "I shall not want."

[1] "A Child of the King" by Harriet E. Buell.
[2] See Appendix for a list of 101 Volunteer Careers in the Local Church.

chapter eight

Your Undivided Attention, Please!

(Revelation—Reception—Redemption)

James 1:19-25

"Guard your steps when you go to the house of God. Go near to listen rather than to offer the sacrifice of fools, who do not know that they do wrong" (Ecclesiastes 5:1, NIV). King Solomon said a mouthful (wrote a scrollful?) there! How did he know we would need to be cautioned against glib, presumptuous worship? Old King Sol possessed God-given wisdom (1 Kings 3:11, 12) that gave him unusually perceptive insights about human nature—that's how!

Many of Solomon's sage sayings have been paraphrased in colloquial terminology, and are widely used even by folk who have no idea that their aphorisms are Biblical in origin. If the quotation above were put in abbreviated contemporary parlance, it might say, "One learns more by listening than by talking." (Check the verses immediately following the one quoted.)

Unfortunately, neither Joe nor Jane Christian is naturally inclined to be a good listener. Both are about as likely to *listen* in the house of God as they are to *think*—and that isn't very. The call to worship, the prayers, the meditations, the anthems, and three-fourths of the sermon may go in one ear and out the other. Worshipers sorely need to tune in their "receivers" to hear and understand God who *reveals* himself to those who seek Him.

God's revelation: that should be enough stimulus to "hook" a positive response of open-minded attention. When He speaks, why doesn't everyone sit up and listen?

Christianity is *revealed* religion. God's gift of revelation renders Jehovah-worship unique. Both the written Word (2 Peter 1:20, 21) and the living Word (John 1:1-14) were sent by God to let man know who He is, to tell what He's like, and to inform us of His plan and purpose. Ours is no mystery religion, for we are privileged to share God's secrets of the ages (Romans 16:25, 26). We don't have to walk, or worship, in the dark, for life with God is illuminated by truth (Psalm 119:105).

The worship transaction is incomplete without this vital exchange stimulated by God's revelation. Our weekly assemblies originated with people who were intensely committed to God's Word, living and written. The holy Scriptures were read, revered, and remembered. They were preached and taught, memorized and recited. The "sacred oracles" provide the purpose, the program, and the promises that are part and parcel of genuine worship.

Public reading and exposition of the Scriptures are still vital components to be included in the proceedings of any formal worship gathering in God's name. He still speaks to us through the Word; indeed, He has elected "by the foolishness of preaching to save them that believe" (1 Corinthians 1:21). There is no salvation without believing, no believing without hearing, no hearing without preaching (Romans 10:13-17).

58

Jesus underlined the importance of God's revelation when He said, "Ye shall know the truth, and the truth shall make you free" (John 8:32). The ultimate reason why God reveals His truth to man is man's *redemption*. [Now don't worry this time if the horse seems to be pushing the cart in our analysis. God's gifts of revelation and redemption are so closely linked that rearranging the outline to consider them together is justified. Discussion of the worshiper's response will come a few paragraphs further on.]

When divine revelation is freely received, God's counter-response in the transaction is redemption— salvation (Romans 10:13-17). Paul traces the conviction/conversion process all the way back to the word of God. Exposure to God's truth is the necessary starting place for the Christian pilgrimage. Recharging the spiritual battery at regular intervals is recommended maintenance for Christians who desire to grow and go for God. "The gospel . . . is the power of God unto salvation" (Romans 1:16).

Obviously Joe and Jane Christian (average latter-day worshipers) do not attach redemptive significance to Biblical preaching and teaching. They frequently forsake the assembly for as shallow an excuse as vacation travel or entertaining relatives. They rarely, if ever, miss a *meal* for those reasons (or for any other reason, come to think of it), but they never think seriously about such inconsistencies in their value system. It seems to have never occurred to them that spiritual food is far more vital to their well-being than physical food.

Even when Joe and Jane are in attendance at worship, their attention to the truth that makes them free is often less than undivided. And their appetites and tastes are underdeveloped and uncultured. They are never very "hungry," yet their lack of appetite is not usually due to "in-between-meal snacks." They prefer sugary platitudes washed down with skim-milk reviews of familiar Bible stories further diluted by amusing anecdotes and catch phrases. They want to be entertained more than they want to be fed; they value amusement more than nourishment.

Perhaps the *foolishness* of preaching is that so few ever hear it. Central to the worship transaction stimulated by divine revelation is the *reception* of truth by which one is redeemed. That is why James exhorts his readers to be "swift to hear ... and receive with meekness the engrafted word, which is able to save your souls" (James 1:19-21).

Joe and Jane and you and I are not too swift at hearing. We are far more adept at speaking: declaring, complaining, wishing, defending, accusing, asking, whispering, back-talking, slandering, arguing, profaning, blaspheming—words, words, words! Our mouths are motorized and our ears are cauterized. The contemporary church has trained preachers (to her credit), but she has not trained *hearers.* Twenty years in the pulpit have convinced me that Christians should be taught how to *hear.*

One of my favorite stories is about the eager young insurance salesman trying to sell a policy to an elderly couple. He used statistics, jokes, tear-jerking illustrations—every method of persuasion in which he had been carefully trained. He waxed eloquent for fifteen minutes, then looked the old man straight in the eye and waited for a response. The prospect simply sat, silently returning the gaze of the salesman without a word.

After several painful minutes of silence the young eager beaver launched into his pitch again, reviewing in detail the provisions and benefits of the insurance policy. When he paused to wait for the old man's reaction, again there was *silence.* In desperation, the rookie salesman turned to the lady of the house.

60

"What else can I say? I've covered every detail and answered every possible objection—I've made this policy as plain as A-B-C!"

"Yes," the old lady agreed, "but Grandpa is D-E-F!"

The gospel has been preached and taught for centuries by scores of ministers who have made it as clear as A-B-C. But the vast majority of the worldwide audience have responded as if they were "D-E-F." Jesus described them when He quoted Isaiah: "This people's heart is waxed gross, and their ears are dull of hearing" (Matthew 13:15). A few parables later in that passage, Jesus is recorded as saying, "Who hath ears to hear, let him hear" (v. 43). Christian stewardship involves the ears we are given just as surely as it involves the wealth we are given.

Though the type of hearing that Jesus commanded involves far more than simple auditing, the response *does begin* with listening. Someone attending a large gathering of religious-political zealots commented to a friend, "Most of these guys look like you'd have to smack 'em between the eyes with a two-by-four to get their attention!" It is, of course, the responsibility of any speaker to hook the attention of his audience. On the other hand, the audience must accept the reciprocal responsibility of *giving* attention.

Joe and Jane Christian would marvel at the attention span of the Hebrew ex-exiles whose listening endurance is described in Nehemiah 8. When Ezra and the priests read the law of God, "from the morning until midday . . . the ears of the people were attentive." A very few minutes is all that modern worshipers seemingly can endure, and even then they are easily distracted. Listening is an art, a lost art that deserves rediscovery.

The second step in spiritual hearing is *testing.* "Take heed what ye hear," Jesus warns (Mark 4:24). "Prove all things; hold fast that which is good," Paul

61

agrees (1 Thessalonians 5:21). In less formal language, the Bible is telling us, "Don't believe everything you hear."

Jane and Joe too typically extend *carte blanche* pulpit privileges to their preacher, accepting whatever he says without question. Unlike their New Testament forerunners, they have not exercised the gift of spiritual discernment (Acts 17:11, NIV).

To hear truth properly, you must discipline yourself by study so you will know how to identify the truth. You must train yourself to recognize the gospel and to detect false doctrine. (It isn't necessary to become a "heresy hunter" who wields the sword of the Spirit irresponsibly at innocent expositors.) And you must become selective in the opinions that you "amen" or applaud. The truth of a statement is not determined by noting the decibel level at which it is spoken. No preacher or teacher should get points for sheer volume. Objective testing for truth by reference to God's written revelation is required of those who would be "swift to hear."

The most important requirement of hearing the truth, however, is your *response.* How do you react to sermons and lessons, to Bible study and inspirational reading? My father used to say (sometimes rather loudly), when I had failed repeatedly to respond to a request, *"Dick, did you hear me?"* He knew, of course, that my ears had received the message, that his request had been transmitted through hammer, anvil, and stirrup from my eardrums. What he was really wondering was why I had not moved in quick compliance. It is totally just that I should now experience the same frustration with my own children.

My father, my brother, two brothers-in-law, and I are preachers, so we also experience a similar frustration when response to preaching and teaching is not immediately perceptible. We want to shout to our respective congregations, "Did you hear me? Did you hear what God is saying to you through His Word, through His servant?" And they, like disobedient children, would understand the other questions implied: "Why haven't you responded? Why don't you do what God wants you to do? Why don't you become what God wants you to be?"

The prophets of old grew impatient with the same kind of apathy, lip service, and mere intellectual assent. God spoke to Ezekiel about his congregation: "They come ... and they sit ... and they hear thy words, but they will not do them: for with their mouth they show much love, but their heart goeth after their covetousness" (Ezekiel 33:31).

James spoke to the same problem in the New Testament church: "Be ye doers of the word, and not hearers only, deceiving your own selves" (James 1:22). Spiritual hearing (reception of revealed truth for redemption) includes listening, testing, and positive responses. "He that hath an ear, let him hear what the Spirit saith unto the churches" (Revelation 2:7).

chapter nine

Don't Just Sit on the Premises!

(Promises—Promises—Promises)

Hebrews 1:6-12

On the dining-room table in some Christian homes is a small box containing a hundred or so multi-colored cards on each one of which is printed a Scripture verse. Each verse reveals a promise of God—to His people, to His children, to His church. Here are some of them.

If from thence thou shalt seek the Lord thy God, thou shalt find him (Deuteronomy 4:29).

Wait on the Lord: be of good courage, and he shall strengthen thine heart (Psalm 27:14).

Your heart shall live that seek God (Psalm 69:32).

The Lord is nigh unto all them that call upon him, to all that call upon him in truth. He will fulfil the desire of them that fear him: he also will hear their cry, and will save them (Psalm 145:18, 19).

Those that seek me early shall find me (Proverbs 8:17).

64

Look unto me, and be ye saved, all the ends of the earth (Isaiah 45:22).

Ask, and it shall be given you; seek, and ye shall find; knock, and it shall be opened unto you (Luke 11:9).

Him that cometh to me I will in no wise cast out (John 6:37).

Draw nigh to God, and he will draw nigh to you (James 4:8).

If any man hear my voice, and open the door, I will come in to him, and will sup with him, and he with me (Revelation 3:20).

Once a day, when the family is seated at the table for a meal, Mom, Dad, or one of the kids takes a card from the box and reads aloud one of the promises of God. Then the family may sing a gospel chorus, review their prayer list, and join hands while one of them leads in a prayer of praise, petition, and promise.

Promises always seem to hook your *Child.* Children dote on promises. Behavior can be surprisingly modified by a conditional promise.

"If you will make your bed and straighten your room, we will go to McDonalds for lunch."

"We may go to the circus on Saturday if you kids will not fight over the TV for the rest of the week."

"Bring home straight A's next quarter, and we'll shop for some wheels of your own!"

Such promises only work, of course, if the parent has proven trustworthy in past experience. (Most of us would sacrifice nearly anything to keep a promise to those we love.) If promises to a child have been repeatedly broken, he will not respond positively to the stimulus.

Father God keeps His promises. He founded His family by establishing a covenant. He renewed that promise to each generation of the covenant people,

65

and proved trustworthy in every age. The *new* covenant (New Testament) is God's conditional agreement with "new Israel"—all the redeemed in Christ.

In the worship transaction, we respond to the promises of God's presence, power, and providence. We adore Him, confess to Him, petition Him, sacrifice to Him—all that we may renew and sustain the salvation covenant. We know that God will keep His promises, for our Heavenly Father has never failed us yet, and we trust the truth of His immutability—He will not change. In Him our present welfare and our future salvation are secure.

The love and loyalty of children to parents is born and nurtured by past promises *kept,* present promises *anticipated,* and future promises *implied.* Some promises are unspoken, yet understood. Shelter, warmth, food, clothing, safety—these are family benefits and the renewal of promises. Each meal promises another; each day of warmth and safety lifts subconscious hope for another; and each act of love and acceptance is interpreted by a trusting child as "earnest" for more and more of the same.

Children of God stand on His promises. (Unfortunately, some seem more inclined to "sit on the premises," unmoved by God's faithfulness.) We also bow, kneel, and march forward on His promises. We anchor and rest there too. We worship, whether alone, with family, or in public assembly, *expectantly,* for we are

Standing on the promises that cannot fail,
When the howling storms of doubt and fear assail;
. . . Standing on the promises of God.
                                        —R. Kelso Carter

When a child is hooked by the stimulus of a promise, he is quick to reciprocate with promises of his own.

"McDonalds? My bed will be made and my room will be straightneed in a flash!"

"Sure, we'll agree on which programs to watch; we won't fight; we won't fight!"

"All *right!* For a car of my own I'll even study on weekends to get straight A's!"

When God hooks your *Child* with the stimulus of His promises, your response is in terms of your own promises. In other words, you resolve to fulfill the conditions of His covenant. "Yes, Lord, I will draw near and stay near; I will shun all other gods and reject all other masters; I will abstain from even the appearance of evil; I will be a faithful steward; etc., etc., etc."

Like Jacob, we go "back to Bethel" to renew our vows before God (Genesis 35), and God counterresponds with renewal of His covenant—more *promises!*

I will give peace in the land (Leviticus 26:6).

The Lord thy God will set thee on high above all nations (Deuteronomy 28:1).

He will keep the feet of his saints (1 Samuel 2:9).

He that trusteth in the Lord, mercy shall compass him about (Psalm 32:10).

Thou hast been faithful over a few things, I will make thee ruler over many things (Matthew 25:21).

I am with you alway, even unto the end of the world (Matthew 28:20).

Whosoever shall lose his life for my sake and the gospel's, the same shall save it (Mark 8:35).

He that believeth on the Son hath everlasting life (John 3:36).

I will come again, and receive you unto myself (John 14:3).

All things work together for good to them that love God (Romans 8:28).

To him that overcometh will I give to eat of the tree of life, which is in the midst of the paradise of God (Revelation 2:7).

Now those are promises you can take to the bank! You can live by them, worship by them, serve by them, and die by them. You can arise and live forever according to the promises of God. Therein lies our blessed assurance.

There's no disappointment in Jesus,
He's all that He promised to be;
His love and His care comfort me everywhere;
He is no disappointment to me.

—John C. Hallett[1]

Come to the Nitty Gritty

(Call—Commitment—Commission)

Matthew 11:28-30

Public worship is properly punctuated, after exhortation from the Word, by a formal invitation to *accept, receive, trust, obey,* and *follow* Christ. (There are very likely other words as well to describe the attitude and action necessary to bring one into a saved relationship with God through Jesus, but let these few suffice.) The weekly assembly of the saints is an ideal time, though certainly not the *only* time, for one to give himself to Christ. The more public the decision, the more effectual the witnessing power of commitment.

Response to the Christian invitation is not exclusively the privilege of unforgiven sinners. "Decision time" is also an opportunity for Christians to recommit themselves to Christ and to His kingdom. It is a time for dedication and *re*dedication, for surrender and *re*surrender, for submission and *re*submission. It is a time in public worship when every worshiper participates by yielding a bit more fully and sincerely to the lordship of Christ.

Commitment is the element of worship under analysis in this chapter. It is to the shame of twentieth-century Christianity, and to the impotency of the church, that Joe and Jane Christian know so little about Christian commitment. Too few latter-day disciples have totally surrendered to Jesus as Lord and Master of their existence. Few enough have accepted Christ as Savior; fewer still have recognized Him as *ruler* in personal life. Many who believe He is presently enthroned at God's right hand have never allowed Christ to mount the throne of their hearts. Christian worship from their perspective is distorted and powerless. Worse than that, it is unacceptable to God (Revelation 3:16).

The stimulus in this worship transaction is *God's call*. The divine *Parent* calls your TA *Child* to worship and work, and when you respond with genuine commitment, you become a commissioned officer in God's mighty army.

God's call came in Ur to Abram: "Get thee out of thy country . . . unto a land that I will show thee" (Genesis 12:1). Abraham obeyed, and God "blessed him, and increased him" (Isaiah 51:2).

God's call came in Midian to Moses: "Come now therefore, and I will send thee unto Pharaoh, that thou mayest bring forth my people the children of Israel out of Egypt" (Exodus 3:10). "By faith Moses . . . forsook Egypt" and led the people of God "through the Red Sea as by dry land" (Hebrews 11:24-29).

God's call came in Shiloh to Samuel: "Samuel, Samuel. Then Samuel answered, Speak; for thy servant heareth" (1 Samuel 3:10).

God's call came in Judah to Isaiah: "Whom shall I send, and who will go for us?" Isaiah responded: "Here am I; send me" (Isaiah 6:8).

God's call came in Galilee to Peter and Andrew: "Follow me, and I will make you fishers of men. And

70

they straightway left their nets, and followed him" (Matthew 4:19, 20).

God's call came near Damascus to Saul: "Arise, and go into the city, and it shall be told thee what thou must do." Saul obeyed, and with the remaining years of his life preached Christ's name "before the Gentiles, and kings, and the children of Israel" (Acts 9:6, 15).

God's call comes by His Son to you and to me:

> Jesus calls us; o'er the tumult
> Of our life's wild, restless sea;
> Day by day His sweet voice soundeth,
> Saying, "Christian, follow Me."
> Jesus calls us from the worship
> Of the vain world's golden store,
> From each idol that would keep us,
> Saying, "Christian, love Me more."

Our response is worship if we pray:

> Savior, may we hear thy call;
> Give our hearts to thy obedience,
> Serve and love thee best of all
> —Cecil F. Alexander

Songwriters have dwelt upon God's call and man's commitment:

"Jesus is tenderly calling thee home"

—"I am coming, Lord!"

"All things are ready, come to the feast"

—"Now I'm coming home."

"Softly and tenderly Jesus is calling"

—"O lamb of God, I come!"

The call of God is not only to *salvation,* but to *service* as well. Spiritual songs again verbalize the transaction:

"Go ye into all the world"
—"I'll go where you want me to go, dear Lord."
"Send the light . . . from shore to shore"
—"If Jesus goes with me, I'll go anywhere!"
"Publish glad tidings"
—"We've a story to tell to the nations."
"Rouse, then, soldiers . . . pass the word along"
—"Like a mighty army moves the church of God."

Responding to the invitation of Christ is answering the call of both Savior and Sender, both Redeemer and Recruiter. He is a Commissioner as well as a Converter. He is a Dispatcher as well as a Discipler. And answering the call in any case requires *commitment*.

You already know that our friends Joe and Jane are not big on commitment—that is, when it concerns religion. They signed their names to nearly a dozen forms when they mortgaged their house, but they steadfastly refuse to sign any kind of a pledge or promise for church enterprises. When Joe's boss throws a luau for employees and mates, they RSVP without excuse, and they let nothing conflict with the appointment. On the other hand, having been invited to the Lord's table for a memorial meal planned just for them, Joe and Jane often miss *that* appointment for no reason of significance. In fact, when the Christians are visited by church callers, they usually say something like, "We'll try to be there Sunday—but we won't promise."

What Joe and Jane Christian need desperately to know is that *they have already promised*. When they stepped forward to declare their faith in Christ, when they submitted to Christian baptism, when their names were added to church membership rolls (and more importantly to the Lamb's Book of Life), *then* and *there* they promised to be faithful in worship, blameless in behavior, and zealous in Christian witness. They pledged their tithes and offerings, time and talents, gifts and influence to Christ and to His church. At that very moment they were committing their discipleship, their stewardship, and their fellowship to the Lord Jesus and to the kingdom cause. It was the single most important decision of their lives!

Active Christians must perpetually participate in this worship transaction at the center of which is commitment. Sometimes it is called *consecration.* By whatever name, it is a pledge of allegiance. You promise your loyalty, your love, your very life. You are a "living sacrifice, holy, acceptable unto God, which is your reasonable service" ("spiritual worship"—NIV) (Romans 12:1).

Do you have the capacity for total commitment? Most of us have become unwitting products of a hedging society. Witnesses testify with their fingers crossed. Politicians dodge issues, and dance around questions when the answers might force them from the middle of the road. Preachers leave theological back doors open in case they want to beat a hasty retreat from Christian dogma. These days everyone seems to be waiting to cheer, waiting until the game is nearly over so they can be certain they are rooting for the winners.

Where are the Christians who will take a stand on God's truth and stake their lives on it? Where are soldiers of the cross who will pledge allegiance to the Crucified without reservation? Where are the defenders of the faith who will speak without equivocation where the Bible speaks? Where are the redeemed of the Lord who will say so without trepidation?

God continues to issue His call to all who will drink of the water of life freely (Revelation 22:17), and to all who will share a cool cup in Christ's name (Matthew 10:42); to all who will possess the light of life (John 8:12), and to all who will shine as cities set on a hill (Matthew 5:14); to all who will accept spiritual nourishment from the bread of life (John 6:35), and to all who will supply bread for food to the poor (2 Corinthians 9:10).

When you answer God's call with personal commitment, whether in private or public worship, He will counter your response with a commission beyond your capabilities to fulfill. He will give you an assignment that will take more energy, more ingenuity, more skill, more resources, and more persistence than you can generate. God will challenge every ounce of unselfish ambition in your soul. He will give you a job that will bring you to your knees and make you cry for help. He will assign you a task for which you will need absolutely nothing less than divine assistance—and then He will give you *that* too.

God expects you to win your world for Christ, and He will help you do it (Matthew 28:18, 19). That is why it is called the "Great Commission," and that is why it requires great commitment.

> The God of all grace, who hath called us unto his eternal glory by Christ Jesus, after that ye have suffered a while, make you perfect, stablish, strengthen, settle you (1 Peter 5:10).

chapter eleven

Can't Never
Did Anything

(Tasks—Trust—Transformation)

Philippians 4:10-13

By now you may feel as if you're sinking fast in a sea of "should have," "ought to," and "will you please . . . ?" "I can't do *everything!*" you are tempted to rebel. "I never dreamed that Christian worship is so much like *work!* What do you want from me—blood?" You know, of course, how Jesus would answer that. Drinking from His "cup" and experiencing His "baptism" is the challenge of discipleship (Matthew 20:22).

Your reaction, however, is understandable. You're behaving like a child, your TA *Child.* Children do chafe under a burden of responsibilities, and occasionally even rebel. "I can't" is a fairly typical response of a child who is frustrated by tasks that seem interminable or beyond his ability. Sometimes "I can't" simply means "I don't want to" or "I won't."

But if you sincerely feel you are incapable of doing everything that's expected of a Christian, you are stepping in the right direction. Your assessment is totally accurate; you *alone* can never hope to accomplish what God requires. Think of it:

Worship (public, private, family, etc.)
Witness (your private world and the "uttermost")
Minister (counseling, benevolence, listening)
Teach (family, classes, "all nations")
Serve (volunteer careers, community, good citizenship)

There's no end to the list; it's utterly overwhelming!

Remember how your parents, instructors, and other concerned adults tried to persuade you to throw *can't* out of your vocabulary? We've all heard the story of the little train who thought he could—and *did.* We may even be *weary* of hearing it. After all, an anthropomorphized train really stretches the imagination.

On the other hand, the apostle Paul *captures* our imagination with his positive expression regarding the work and works of Christianity. Can you catch his faithful optimism? "I can do all things through Christ which strengtheneth me" (Philippians 4:13).

There is the secret of successful discipleship! Even against insurmountable odds, you can do everything—if you let Christ help. Would you agree that it is not humanly possible for one man to do in such a short time all that Paul accomplished in the few years following his conversion? Of course it isn't possible! Paul had help: divine strength supplied through an intimate relationship with his Savior and Lord.

Are you wondering why we're even discussing this in a book that purports to be about *worship?* Let me remind you of our working definition: "Christian worship is a divine/human transaction stimulated by God and His gifts, rendered by man in attitudes and actions, and reciprocated by God with rich rewards for those who diligently seek Him." There is nothing in that to restrict its application to acts of formal, public assemblies and ceremonies. Webster even agrees that worship is any "act expressing reverence to a divine being."

You see, every aspect of your existence can and should render reverence to God. Your whole life, as it is lived moment to moment, day after day, can become one perpetual symphony of praise, ongoing obeisance before your Maker and Master. A living sacrifice is your "spiritual worship" (Romans 12:1, NIV). Worship that never makes it beyond the inside of the church-house door, that is never expressed in obedient service by Christians "in the world but not of the world," must be what Solomon called the "sacrifice of fools" (Ecclesiastes 5:1). Therefore we will now consider this transaction that is stimulated by the challenge of God's work to which Christians must respond with trusting obedience.

Parents know that their children usually tackle chores with much greater enthusiasm when Mom and/or Dad give a hand in the work. (Leaders of adults know that the same principle applies to *their* activities.) How much more our Heavenly Father is willing to give His children a helping hand in doing the work to which He has called us! We can do all things because Christ strengthens us.

When you determine to arise early every morning for private personal prayer, God will give you the willpower to keep that resolve. When you make or take opportunities to speak a good word about Christ to a friend or neighbor (even a stranger or an enemy), God will give you the right words to say. When you consent to serve "above and beyond the call of duty," God will give you the extra energy and whatever else you need to complete the task. When you comfort the bereaved, counsel the troubled, visit a prisoner or a dying friend, God will give you courage. He will minister to individual needs through your concern and your presence as well as through your words. If you make an effort to teach your children "the way," God will inspire your lessons and become real to your pupils. God will help!

Joe and Jane Christian have some mental reservations about that. Theirs is a *believing* faith, but not necessarily a *trusting* faith. They pride themselves upon being "realistic" and "pragmatic." They have read all the books on self-assertiveness, looking out for oneself, intimidation, saying "no," and "doing it my way." They are close to becoming members of the "I" cult—humanists who believe and promote a subjective, selfish, godless philosophy.

Most of the Joes and Janes in modern Christendom are not aware that they have embraced humanistic, existential doctrines. They would most certainly be hard-pressed to define those terms. But still they seem to be outgrowing their trust in a God who is active in human affairs. They would *rather do it themselves.*

Having been thus victimized by fashionable philosophical fads, average Christians schedule and budget their time, make daily lists of priorities, delegate authority, "sub-contract" details, take generous doses of Geritol and/or Valium, grit their teeth, and run off in several directions at once to do their "church work"—but do not ask or expect divine help. It is no wonder that the *work of the church* is not being done. Independence, ignorance, cynicism, and selfish pride have disempowered the body.

When confronted by gargantuan tasks of Christian discipleship, your best response is *trust*—trust in God, who is your "refuge and strength" (Psalm 46:1), and in Christ, whose "yoke is easy" and whose "burden is light" (Matthew 11:30). Jesus promises spiritual rest for the hurried and harried, the frustrated and frazzled. The only condition is "come unto me"—but too many believers rather pop a pill.

The apostle Paul had learned that Christ can be trusted for added strength when it is needed—enough to do "all things" (Philippians 4:13). His testimony is meaningful because he had repeatedly put that truth to the test. "We are troubled on every side, yet not distressed; we are perplexed, but not in despair; persecuted, but not forsaken; cast down, but not destroyed" (2 Corinthians 4:8, 9).

If Paul had written that passage nineteen hundred years later, I wonder if he would have prefaced those verses thus: "Due to my personal assertiveness, positive thinking, willpower, industry, and pure grit, I have achieved, endured, survived. . . ." No, I am confident Paul would credit his success with the same sentiments, if not the same words, he wrote in the first century. "We have this treasure in jars of clay to show that this all-surpassing power is from God and not from us" (2 Corinthians 4:7, NIV).

Your power to perform God-given tasks is supplied from an outside Source. If you insist on tugging at your own bootstraps to become what God wants you to be and to accomplish what God wants you to do, surely guilt and immaturity shall plague you all the days of your life, and you will dwell in the house of failure forever.

The secret word here is trust—worship at its best. You know that God can help you make time in your busy days for kingdom work—believe that He *will*. You know that God can use your personality to influence others for Christ and the church—believe that He *will*. You know that God can give you the right words to say in a witnessing conversation—believe that He *will*. You know that God can supply a "second wind" when you become "weary in well-doing"—believe that He *will*. You know God can literally transform you by the "renewing of your mind"—believe that He *will*.

That is how God empowers Christians to do all His will. He transforms us, when we respond to the challenge of His tasks with trust. When a convert surrenders all his soul, heart, mind, and strength to the Lord, you can count on it—some changes are going to be made! Paul describes that transformation more than once in his letters to growing Christians. To the Colossians, for example, he wrote, "You have taken off your old self with its practices and have put on the new self, which is being renewed in knowledge in the image of its Creator" (Colossians 3:9, 10, NIV). His letter to Ephesus includes an identical thought: "You were taught . . . to put off your old self . . . to be made new in the attitude of your minds; and to put on the new self, created to be like God in true righteousness and holiness" (Ephesians 4:22-24, NIV).

Humans who are adopted into the family of God are new creatures in Christ (2 Corinthians 5:17). To them Paul says, "Be ye transformed by the renewing of your mind" (Romans 12:2). Divine transformation comes about when *your mind is changed.* Christian conversion is contingent upon one's changing his mind. Instead of mere alterations in the existing gray matter, a total transplant is prescribed. "Let this mind be in you, which was also in Christ Jesus" (Philippians 2:5).

It all boils down to this: worship that extends itself beyond the closet and the sanctuary is stimulated by the **tasks** to which God calls Christians out from the world. (The Greek word for church—*ekklesia*—means "called-out ones".) Central to the transaction thus initiated is the response of **trust**—leaning on the enabling power of God through Christ. **Transformation** is the divine counter-response that completes the transaction by changing the mind of the worshiper from pride to humility, and from rebellion to obedience. ("There's no other way to be happy in Jesus but to trust and obey.")

> For we are God's workmanship, created in Christ Jesus to do good works, which God prepared in advance for us to do (Ephesians 2:10, NIV).

chapter twelve

More Than Just a Cup of Coffee

(Fellowship—Followership—Fellowship)

Philippians 2:1-11

As Joe and Jane Christian were putting on their coats after early evening worship last Sunday, their friends, the Comonovers, joined them in the foyer. True to their name, they said, "Why don't you come on over for some fellowship?" Joe and Jane were quick to accept the invitation; the Comonovers have a lovely home and always serve such good things to eat!

On the way to the Comonover's residence Joe speculated as to what treats were in store. "I'm starved! I hope they have more than just sweet stuff. Maybe they'll fix sloppy Jims. . . ."

"Don't you mean *sloppy Joes?*" Jane corrected.

"No, *sloppy Jims,*" Joe insisted. "I've always hated that other name. I don't know why someone wanted to pick on us Joes anyway. I hope they have heavenly-goo dessert too—but *after* the sandwiches and chips."

"I'm sure they'll have plenty of goodies; we always have such fun eating at the Comonovers. I'm glad they invited us; I really didn't know what we were going to eat at home tonight anyway."

Jane and Joe weren't surprised to see several familiar cars parked in front of Comonover's house. Their hosts were generous to a fault, and considered Christian hospitality a ministry of stewardship. The house door was ajar just a bit, and pleasant sounds of conversation and laughter invited the Christians inside.

When they had discarded their coats in the front bedroom, Joe and Jane joined the other guests in the family room, where they were welcomed with cordial, if rowdy, greetings. The whole gang was there, and now that everyone had arrived, they sat expectantly, awaiting the scrumptious food that would surely be served shortly.

Finally Jim Comonover stood, as if for attention, and everyone quickly quieted, guessing that the host was about to say "thanks" for the food. Instead Jim cleared his throat and began to make an informal speech.

"You're probably wondering why we invited you all here," he quipped. The gang chuckled, not knowing what to expect next. They were totally unprepared for what Jim was about to say.

"We invited you over tonight for some Christian fellowship—and I guess you might decide that we had ulterior motives. I hope you won't think we tricked you. We really aren't just trying to be cute and clever. And I promise not to preach a sermon." Jim paused for a moment, and Joe shot a quizzical glance at Jane. *What's happening here?* he thought. *I'm hungry, let's eat!*

"I just want to share a few ideas that have come to me in Bible study lately—then we have some activities planned that we hope you'll enjoy." Jim took a deep breath and plunged on.

"It dawned on me the other day that Christian fellowship is much more than just a cup of coffee. Oh, I like 'eatin' meetin's' as well as anyone, and there is certainly New Testament precedent for that kind of fellowship. But the first-century church shared far more than food and fun. They were a close-knit body of believers who 'had everything in common.' They shared in the fellowship of *prayer,* the fellowship of *giving,* the fellowship of *evangelism,* and often in the fellowship of *suffering.* We, on the other hand, have limited our experience of Christian fellowship to an occasional cup of coffee and a monthly carry-in dinner.''

By now several guests were becoming restless; some seemed to be squirming in their seats. Joe's stomach growled, and he quickly cleared his throat to cover up. Jane slammed an elbow into his ribs. He frowned at her, then returned his attention to Jim, who was beginning to outline the plans for the rest of the evening.

"I've been wanting to survey our neighborhood ever since we moved here, to find out who people are and where, or *if,* they worship regularly. With this crowd we can complete the census in an hour or so. We have street maps with assigned areas for each couple, information sheets to fill out, and church-visitation brochures to leave at each home. At 9:30 we will all come back here to compile the results and share our experiences over refreshments.''

Many of the Comonover's guests were in a state of shock. But no one disagreed with what Jim had said, and every couple accepted a survey assignment. They were soon walking the streets of the community, two by two, knocking on doors, speaking a good word for Christ's church, and securing information that would become the seed for a file of prospective Christians to be discipled by the local church.

When the teams reassembled, they were bubbling with enthusiasm and everybody wanted to talk at once. In the excitement, Mrs. Comonover nearly forgot to serve the coffee, hot chocolate, and other goodies she had prepared. But everyone seemed less interested in eating than in sharing their experiences. Even Joe and Jane were for the first time thrilling to the satisfaction of having gone into their private world for Christ and His church.

Later, as the group shared prayer requests, it was reported that one family in the congregation was in financial straits. Almost spontaneously, a hat was passed and a sizeable offering was received to help the needy family. Jim would deliver the money the next day. The evening ended with the whole gang making a prayer circle, hands clasped and hearts overflowing from the new experiences of Christian fellowship at its best.

Joe and Jane were so stimulated when they finally got back home that they couldn't get to sleep right away. Jane finished a book she was reading while Joe made a Dagwood sandwich they could share. They both agreed just before they finally dozed off that this had been the most enjoyable evening they ever had shared with Christian friends.

Jim Comonover had reached some of his "revolutionary" conclusions as he read the book of Philippians. The apostle Paul, through inspiration of the Holy Spirit, reveals several insights concerning Christian fellowship in that letter. He writes of "fellowship in the gospel" (1:5), "fellowship of the Spirit" (2:1), "fellowship of sufferings" (3:10), as well as fellowship in "my affliction" (4:14-16).

Paul is teaching that Christian fellowship is a *partnership* for the furtherance of the gospel. It is *communion* with the Holy Spirit. It sometimes means sharing the burden and hurt of Christ. And it also expresses itself in *communication* with family needs.

That is descriptive of the *koinonia* possessed by the first Christians, the New Testament church. Acts 2:42

reports that they "continued steadfastly in *fellowship*" (among other things.) Many folk regard the items listed in that verse as an informal agenda of worship in the early church. Whether that is a proper interpretation or not, it is clear that fellowship is the "tie that binds our hearts in Christian love."

God stimulates the worship transaction under consideration here by *giving* to His children this cohesive dynamic called fellowship. W. Carl Ketcherside insists that it is a gift: "The *koinonia* to which we have been called of God is one of the Spirit. It is not a fellowship created by human agency. It cannot be legislated by a convention nor can it be conferred by a conference. It can be enjoyed, but not enjoined. The Holy Spirit produces, promotes, and protects this fellowship."[1]

The response of a Christian worshiper to God's gift of fellowship may be called *followership.* Yes, that word is in the dictionary. Webster defines it as "the capacity or willingness to follow a leader."[2] Worship is an expression of that capacity and of that willingness.

Although fellowship is certainly not limited to what happens at our weekly public assemblies, Christians should sense it and share it there in a unique fashion. It is in public worship that we experience corporately the "joy divine" of "leaning on the everlasting arms." It is there too that we recommit ourselves, individually and unitedly, to the special family fraternity into which we have been called by our faith in Christ.

That explains why the writer of the Biblical letter to the Hebrews is dogmatic when he says, "Let us not give up meeting together, as some are in the habit of doing, but let us encourage one another" (Hebrews 10:25, NIV). He prefaced that exhortation by stating some significant reasons for "meeting together": 1) to draw near to God; 2) to be reassured in our faith; 3) to get a fresh hold on hope; and 4) to "consider how we may spur one another on toward love and good deeds'' (vv. 22-24). The next verses elaborate the spiritual jeopardy of apostasy, and thus imply yet another important reason for faithfulness in followership.

The counter-response of God in this transaction is another kind of fellowship—human/divine fellowship. Jesus has promised, ''Where two or three are gathered together in my name, there am I in the midst of them'' (Matthew 18:20).

A special divine presence is visited upon two or three, or two or three hundred, who are assembled (gathered, worshiping, sharing fellowship, expressing followership) in the name of Christ. And that kind of fellowship should put another song in your heart:

A blessed fellowship my soul has found
With Him whose sweetest name is love;
In Christ the riches of God's grace abound,
The joys eternal from above.

When I'm with Him, when I'm with Him,
The fairest pleasures of the world grow dim;
And in my heart I feel the thrill of glory;
When I'm with Him, when I'm with Him.[3]

[1]Mission Messenger, 1963, p. 98.
[2]Webster's New Collegiate Dictionary
[3] ''When I'm With Him'' Copyright 1939, The Rodeheaver Co. © Renewed 1967, The Rodeheaver Co. All Rights Reserved. International copyright secured. Used by Permission.

chapter thirteen

Put It All in One Word!

(Love—Love—Love)

1 John 4:16-21

You might have known it would come to this! When the transactions of Christian worship are reduced (or should we say *magnified?*) to a common denominator, that factor is *love.* I am almost reluctant to mention it, because you know all there is to know about love—right? I mean, your first Bible memory verse was probably John 3:16, and you must have heard explanations of the Greek terms for *love* at least a dozen times. In fact, the name of your class or congregation may be *Agape.* You've heard all of your preacher's best illustrations of *love;* dozens of songs in your hymnbooks are about *love;* and the last six retreats you attended featured in-depth studies of 1 John. You may be so tired of hearing *love, love,* love that you're threatening to sell your tennis racket!

Before you tear out this last chapter, give just a few more minutes' consideration to something that will make your worship much better for you. That *is* what you want, isn't it? You want worship to be *better,* not boring.

Why is it that Jane and Joe Christian are rather bored with worship? Several possible reasons suggest themselves. Average worshipers are not usually *prepared* for worship. Some wise observer said, "He prays best in public who prays often in private." A person who does not live his life in an attitude of prayer and worship will find it difficult to jump into that mood on Sunday morning. (Practical preparations such as sufficient Saturday-night rest and adequate time for dressing and eating Sunday morning are important too.)

Almost everyone knows that realization of benefits from any experience varies in direct proportion to the degree of personal involvement. Some folk are disenchanted with public worship simply because they have *quit worshiping!* They may still be in regular attendance at the weekly assembly, but they merely warm the pew, go through the motions, and fail to respond spiritually to God's gifts.

The detriment of disproportionate emphasis upon the *subjective* has already been elaborated in another chapter. The problem is so universally prevalent, however, that repetition is justified. Worshipers must fix their minds upon God, not upon their own feelings, if the Lord's Day experience is to be a meaningful one.

Andrew Blackwood distilled this truth in one paragraph of his book, *The Fine Art of Worship:*

Whenever we mortals worship God, the determining factor is his character. Sometimes we think more about matters of time and place, rites and ceremonies, than we think about him. With the woman at the well, to whom the Lord Jesus explained the meaning of public worship, we need to learn that where anyone has the will to worship God, he is waiting to show that person how; and that where the will to worship is not present, all our human devices are but as sounding brass and tinkling cymbal. "God is a Spirit: and they that worship him must worship him in spirit and in truth"; that is, our worship must be sincere, and it must be real. Here, then, should be our emphasis, "Worship Him!"[1]

Genuine worship is an expression of love for God in response to love from God. "We love him, because he first loved us" (1 John 4:19). Joe and Jane and you and I will be stimulated to worship God when we concentrate upon "his great love wherewith he loved us" (Ephesians 2:4).

> Love divine, all loves excelling,
> Joy of heav'n, to earth come down;
> Fix in us Thy humble dwelling;
> All Thy faithful mercies crown.
> Jesus, Thou art all compassion,
> Pure, unbounded love Thou art;
> Visit us with Thy salvation;
> Enter every trembling heart.
> —Charles Wesley

The love of God has not gone totally unrequited, for worshipers through the centuries have loved Him back. Perhaps one reason people get bored in worship, and feel "unfulfilled" upon leaving the church house, is that they, like the Christians at Ephesus, have left their first love (Revelation 2:4). It is important to remember that Christians do what they do on Sunday, or any other day for that matter, because they love God. Now, love is an emotion, but far more. A meaningful chorus says it this way:

> Love is something you do;
> Love is something you do,

Not always something that you feel,
But it's real!
Love is something you do;
Love is something you do,
When Jesus Christ is living in you.

(Author unknown

The same idea was taught by Christ when He said, "If ye love me, keep my commandments" (John 14:15). Everyone knows in his heart of hearts that true love requires more than lip service. We all *know* it, but more than a few still try to get by on "faith without works." And James reminds us that profession without practice is dead (James 2:17). So that's why worship seems dull and empty for Joe and Jane—*rigor mortis* has set in!

The Greeks are not the only ones who have several words with which to translate *love.* In plain English, love is *respect* (fear, reverence); love is *honor;* love is *gratitude,* love is *obedience,* love is *service.* Love is singing songs of praise; love is giving sacrificial offerings; love is faithfully keeping the memorial of Christ; love is hearing and heeding the Word; love is ministering to the needs of the "least of these" brethren in the name of Jesus. Love is *worship.*

In this transaction of Christian worship God provides the stimulus of love, even though you are *not OK.* You respond in kind with love from your TA *Child* (You're OK; I'm not OK). By God's grace and through the shed blood of Christ, you are then seen as spiritually OK, and God perpetuates the transaction by counter-responding with even *more* divine love.

"Therefore, since we have been justified through faith, we have peace with God through our Lord Jesus Christ . . . because God has poured out his love into our hearts by the Holy Spirit, whom he has given us" (Romans 5:1, 5, NIV).

The Heavenly Father is more than generous with His love, never withholding from those who diligently seek Him. Your worship experience should be a love feast, an *agape* celebration. Interchange of love *revealed* and love *expressed* and love *poured out* is the purpose of coming to His house and gathering in His name. How can anyone be bored with that?

Can you get excited about assembling with the saints on Sunday? Remember, "neither death nor life, neither angels nor demons, neither the present nor the future, nor any powers, neither height nor depth, nor anything else in all creation [*including dragged-out songs, tedious announcements, discordant choirs, lengthy prayers, and poor preaching*], will be able to separate us from the love of God that is in Christ Jesus our Lord" (Romans 8:38, 39, NIV).

[1] Abingdon Press. Used by Permission.

Appendix

101 Volunteer Careers in the Local Church

1. Announcement maker
2. Athlete (church leagues)
3. Athletic director
4. Audio/visual librarian
5. Auditor of church books
6. Baptismal assistant
7. Baptismal garb launderer
8. Baptistry custodian
9. Bulletin board custodian
10. Bus captain
11. Bus driver
12. Camp dorm dean
13. Camp team sponsor
14. Camp teacher
15. Camp waitress
16. Camp "gopher"
17. Choir director
18. Church clerk
19. Church historian
20. Class president
21. Class secretary
22. Class treasurer
23. Committee chairman
24. Committee member
25. Communion steward
26. Corresponding secretary
27. Day-school staffer
28. Day-school superintendent
29. Day-school teacher
30. Deacon
31. Driver (car trips, etc.)
32. Elder
33. Engineer/climate control
34. Evangelistic visitor
35. Financial secretary
36. Floral decorator
37. Food function foreman
38. Greeter at worship

39. Grounds keeper
40. Handbell choir director
41. Handbell ringer
42. Handyperson
43. Hospitality hostess (host)
44. Hospital visitor
45. Hymnal custodian
46. Information desk attendant
47. Instrumentalist
48. Janitor
49. Kitchen custodian
50. Kitchen helper
51. Kitchen supervisor
52. Librarian
53. Lights and locks monitor
54. Light and sound technician
55. Literature distributor
56. Mechanic (church vehicles)
57. Mimeograph operator
58. Minister of benevolence
59. Missions file keeper
60. News correspondent
61. Newsletter editor
62. Newsletter mailing clerk
63. Newsletter typist
64. Nursery attendant
65. Nursery supervisor
66. Offset printer
67. Orchestra director
68. Orchestra musician
69. Organist
70. Photographer
71. Pianist
72. Prayer group leader
73. Projectionist
74. Public relations chairman
75. Purchasing agent
76. Registrar (counter, etc.)
77. Secretary (church office)
78. Shut-in visitor
79. Singer (choir)
80. Singer (solo & ensemble)
81. Song leader
82. Substitute teacher
83. Sunday-school secretary
84. Sunday-school superintendent
85. Sunday-school teacher
86. Survey visitor
87. Team coach (athletics)
88. Telephone chairman
89. Telephone caller
90. Tract-rack custodian
91. Treasurer (church)
92. Trustee
93. Usher
94. Utilities monitor
95. Vacation Bible School craft helper
96. VBS director
97. VBS kitchen steward
98. VBS teacher
99. Volunteer coordinator
100. Worship leader
101. Youth sponsor

Other New Life Books

You may order them from your supplier.

Up From Chaos
by LeRoy Lawson

A study of Genesis unlike any you ever saw before.

The True Life
The Only Way
by Lewis Foster

Twin volumes to deepen your appreciation of the
Gospel of John

After the Spirit Comes
by Roger Thomas

Tracing the dominant themes of the books of Acts

His Way
by Jack Cottrell

A refreshing look at the Ten Commandments and
Christian teaching on the same themes

His Truth
by Jack Cottrell

A profoundly simple presentation
of basic Bible doctrines